The Holy Roman Empire

An Enthralling Overview of One of the Most Powerful European States during the Middle Ages and Early Modern Period

Free limited time bonus

Stop for a moment. We have a free bonus set up for you. The problem is this: we forget 90% of everything that we read after 7 days. Crazy fact, right? Here's the solution: we've created a printable, 1-page pdf summary for this book that you're reading now. All you have to do to get your free pdf summary is to go to the following website: **https://livetolearn.lpages.co/enthrallinghistory/**

Or, Scan the QR code!

Once you do, it will be intuitive. Enjoy, and thank you!

Table of Contents

Introduction

The ascent and downfall of the Holy Roman Empire mark the seemingly universal oscillation of human societies between fragmentation and centralization and between unification and separation. Germanic peoples, who dealt the final blow that brought the Western Roman Empire to its knees, formed a number of new states, which were bound together at one point in the form of Charlemagne's empire. His empire soon perished, and from the ashes rose medieval France and the Holy Roman Empire, both of which were heavily fragmented and lacked central authority. In fact, these medieval states looked nothing like our modern nations.

Even during the most illustrious periods of the Holy Roman Empire, for instance, during the reign of Frederick Barbarossa, the emperor was much less in control of his empire in comparison to modern state administrations. The emperor, of course, almost always had a large army at his disposal, meaning that he could crush those who didn't go along with what he wanted. However, because concepts like nation, state administration, and centralization were virtually nonexistent at the time, it was impossible for the emperor to be in real control of his empire. Practically each emperor of the Holy Roman Empire had to renegotiate the basic terms of his authority with the nobility. The stability of the Holy Roman Empire was dependent on an emperor's ability to be on good terms with their nobles while not giving the nobles too much freedom.

Thus, the Holy Roman Empire, as was the case (and still is to a certain extent) with numerous other states, constantly shifted between periods of relative stability and periods of rebellion against the central authority. The emperor would quench rebellions in one corner of his empire while unrest sprung up elsewhere. So, each emperor had to wage multiple wars, lacking the means to keep his enormous empire fully together.

In a way, the Holy Roman Empire is a historical misnomer. The state was neither holy nor Roman. The adjective "holy" comes from the fact that German emperors were traditionally crowned in Rome. "Roman" comes from the fact that German emperors wanted the same sort of illustriousness enjoyed by the ancient Roman emperors. However, unlike the Roman Empire, the Holy Roman Empire never managed to establish the same centralized administration. During the times of the great Emperor Augustus, Rome had the same sort of state officials and administrative hierarchy across the whole empire, which was even bigger than the Holy Roman Empire. Frederick Barbarossa, on the other hand, arguably the most powerful of all the Holy Roman emperors, was more like a leader of autonomous states (even within modern-day Germany), each having its own laws and power structures. Barbarossa had his own lands and fiefs like his subordinates (vassals). In addition, the Roman Empire had a much more widespread and coherent cultural influence on vast non-Latin areas, whereas the Holy Roman Empire hardly managed to achieve even a fragment of the same kind of influence on non-Germanic areas of their own empire.

This is the main reason for the ultimate dissolution of the Holy Roman Empire after the Peace of Westphalia of 1648. France heralded the birth of a modern nation, while the Germans sank back to the fragmentation and disunity of the pre-empire days. It was only with Bismarck at the helm that Germans could form a single state led by a single, coherent administration.

In this book, we'll deal with the ups and downs of this strange empire. Starting with the fall of the Western Roman Empire, we'll show how Charlemagne's empire was slowly divided into smaller parts, with the Franks on the one hand and the Germans on the other. After describing the days of the first few dynasties that led to the creation of the Holy Roman Empire, we'll spend some time with Barbarossa, following him on his endless conquests and, most importantly, his two crusades. Moving on, we'll show how the Habsburgs gradually took over, leading the state into exceedingly turbulent periods of religious wars and pan-European conflicts.

This book, while being a meticulous collection of the most important facts about the Holy Roman Empire, also provides a deeper explanation of the pitfalls of this mighty and incredibly complex constellation of German states.

Chapter 1: The Genesis of the Holy Roman Empire

Prelude to an Empire

The Holy Roman Empire, like a phoenix, rose from the ashes of the Roman Empire.[1] When the "original" Roman Empire finally collapsed in 476 CE under the burden of barbaric invasions and internal strife, Europe became shrouded in a power vacuum, which was only filled with the gradual formation of the Holy Roman Empire with Charlemagne. But before talking about Charlemagne, one of the greatest emperors to ever live, we'll quickly dissect the fall of the Roman Empire and the power struggle that ensued.

The year 476 brought an end to a once great empire, the Roman Empire. Truth be told, it was only its western part that ceased to exist, as the Eastern Roman Empire continued to exist for another thousand years. However, the city of Rome itself was taken by barbarians, and the Western Roman Empire was dismembered. The invasion of the Huns in the 4th century, spearheaded by Attila, was the final blow to an opponent that was already struggling to stay on its feet. Quickly, over the course of the 5th century, the Western Roman Empire was dismembered by the Ostrogoths, Visigoths, Vandals, Franks, Angles, Saxons, and many others. These Germanic tribes, which had been kept at bay for centuries

---

[1] Heather, Peter. Empires and Barbarians: The Fall of Rome and the Birth of Europe. Oxford University Press, 2010.

by Roman might, spilled over the traditional borders of their states and ventured to new lands.

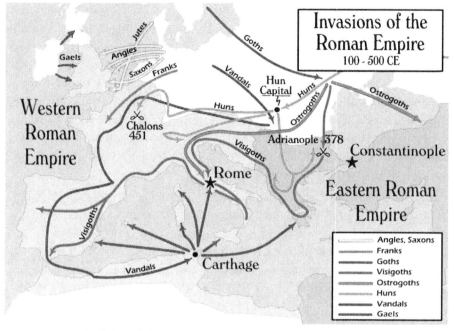

Dissolution of the Roman Empire due to the barbarian invasions
User:MapMaster, CC BY-SA 2.5 <https://creativecommons.org/licenses/by-sa/2.5>, via Wikimedia Commons, https://commons.wikimedia.org/w/index.php?curid=1234669

The Great Migration sets the scene for the formation of the Holy Roman Empire. In fact, the modern landscape of Europe, for the most part, follows the line traced by the Great Migration. And much like our modern democracies draw upon the institutions of ancient Rome, so did the emerging Germanic states after the fall of the Western Roman Empire. Franks, or at least their leaders, believed they had procured their authority and legitimacy not only from God but also from old Roman emperors.

Speaking of God, the Germanic tribes fairly quickly accepted Christianity as their religion, and their successful incorporation of Christianity put them on the lucky side of history. The Eastern Roman Empire, partially thanks to Constantine the Great, who promoted Christianity, showed just how powerful Roman heritage was when coupled with the zeal of Christianity. The Western Roman Empire never seemed to be able to strike this balance.

However, the Germanic states that rose from the ruins of the Western Roman Empire were able to do this. The Franks, after whom modern-day France is named, conquered the old Roman province of Gaul (roughly speaking modern-day France), battling other Germanic tribes. The first Frankish dynasty was the Merovingian dynasty. We don't know too much about the early history of the Merovingian dynasty, but we do know that in the 5th century, they were led by Childeric I and fought other Germanic tribes in Gaul, such as the Visigoths, Burgundians, and others. Childeric I and his subordinates were still pagans. After Childeric I died around 481, his son, Clovis I, took over, finally uniting the Frankish sub-tribes and strengthening his dynasty's position against other Germanic states.

Clovis I married Clotilde, a Burgundian princess who was a Nicene Christian.[2] Eventually, Clovis I accepted the faith of his wife and propagated it to his subordinates, an important decision because most of the Germanic tribes, if baptized, were Arians. Clovis I at least had ideological support from the center of Orthodox Christianity, namely Constantinople. Clovis I chose Paris as the seat of his kingdom in a symbolic way by picking it as his place of burial.

The Merovingian kingdom wasn't stable, and after Clovis I died around 511, his successors vied for supremacy, successfully partitioning the kingdom. Clovis had four sons, so the kingdom was divided into four parts: Austrasia, Neustria, Burgundy, and Aquitaine.[3]

The Merovingian dynasty finally came to an end in the early 8th century. For quite some time, the Merovingian kings were only formally kings; the real power was in the hands of the mayor of the palace, who was, in a way, in charge of the Merovingian royal household. Charles Martel, a Frankish aristocrat, rose to this position in 718 and made way for a new dynasty: the Carolingians.

Charles Martel wasn't simply a court official. He was the de facto head of state and chief military commander. He protected the kingdom from other Germanic states and attempted to unite and enlarge the lands

---

[2] Nicene Christianity was the form of Christianity as defined by the First Council of Nicaea in 325 CE. It stood against Arianism (Arius was an Alexandrine presbyter who emphasized Christ's human nature, believing that Jesus Christ was more a man than a heavenly being and was actually created by God and thus had a beginning and an end).

[3] Contreni, John J. "Introduction: The Merovingian Kingdoms, 450-751." French Historical Studies 19, no. 3 (1996): 755.

conquered by Clovis I. Charles Martel was also instrumental in the defense of Europe from the Umayyad Caliphate.[i] In 732, a decisive battle was fought between the Muslim Umayyads and Germanic peoples: the Battle of Tours (sometimes referred to as the Battle of Poitiers). The Arabs managed to penetrate deep into modern-day France and were only stopped by the forces of Charles Martel and Odo of Aquitaine. From then on, the Muslims were confined to their Hispanic territories, where they stayed for centuries.

After Charles Martel died in 741, the kingdom was divided into two parts. The kingdom was left to his two sons (both de jure mayors of different palaces led by the Merovingians but also de facto rulers), Carloman and Pepin the Short (sometimes referred to as Pepin the Younger). By 747, Pepin the Short had assumed the sole and uncontested supremacy of the land of the Franks, as Carloman decided (or was forced) to become a monk, which was the most convenient way of disposing of unwanted competition. Pepin the Short also dealt with Childeric III, the last Merovingian "king," by sending him to a monastery, where he would spend the remainder of his days without posing a threat to Pepin the Short.

Pepin the Short was the first king of the Carolingian dynasty, gaining support from the archbishop of Mainz, Boniface, in 751. Pepin was anointed by Pope Stephen II in 754. He received the title "Patricius Romanorum," which is an obvious reference to the continuity between the Roman Empire and the Kingdom of the Franks, which we often refer to as the start of the Holy Roman Empire.

Pepin the Short then went about assuring papal supremacy in northern Italy, which had recently been under threat by the Lombards. This is basically how the Papal States were established. The Papal States had an incredibly long lifespan, lasting from 756 all the way to 1870. Pepin also had to battle the Muslims once again, now in Narbonne (southern France), which was recaptured in 759. Pepin died in 768, leaving his kingdom to Charlemagne and Carloman I, with the kingdom once again being divided according to the old Frankish custom.

---

[i] The Umayyad Caliphate is the second caliphate made after the death of Muhammad the Prophet. By 732, the Arabs had reached modern-day Spain and were threatening the Kingdom of the Franks. The Umayyad Caliphate is, territorially speaking, one of the largest empires ever.

As was customary, the two brothers didn't really get along well. There were brief quarrels between Charlemagne's and Carloman's armies, but there wasn't enough time for an all-out war. Carloman I died in 771, and the Kingdom of the Franks was once again unified under one ruler.

Charles the Great

Charles the Great, better known as Charlemagne, was probably born in 742. He was the oldest son of Bertrada and Pepin the Short.[5] Charlemagne also had a younger sister named Gisela, as well as other siblings who probably didn't live long enough to be remembered well by chroniclers.

Charlemagne is well known for his conquests and restless attempts to enlarge his realm. Crucially, he continued the Frankish support of the Papal States, which, by the time of his succession to power in 771, were once again under threat from the Lombards.[6] The Lombardian threat in Italy was silenced by 774, but Charlemagne had to return to Italy in 776 to quench another rebellion.

Charlemagne also continued his father's battle against the Andalusian Muslims. He was able to expand the Frankish realm into modern-day Spain across the Pyrenees. Charlemagne's first campaign here, in 778, almost turned out to be a catastrophe. After being forced to retreat, Charlemagne's forces were ambushed in the Pyrenees, an event that is today known as the Battle of Roncevaux Pass. The Basques ambushed Charlemagne because the two had clashed before, with Charlemagne forcing the Basques into submission. So, the Basques retaliated, and they succeeded in seriously weakening the Frankish forces. Charlemagne got out alive, but many were killed, including people close to Charlemagne, such as a knight named Roland, whose death inspired the *Song of Roland*, one of the very first literary works of art written in French.

Over the next few decades, Charlemagne succeeded in conquering parts of Muslim Andalusia, and by 797, he was able to take Barcelona. Charlemagne was a careful diplomat and was able to make the most of the hostilities between the Umayyads and Abbasids.[7] He had many other

---

[5] Barbero, Alessandro. Charlemagne: Father of a Continent. University of California Press, 2018.

[6] The Lombards were Germanic people who lived in modern-day northern Italy.

[7] In 750, the Umayyads were overthrown by the Abbasids, although Andalusia remained the stronghold of the Umayyads. However, the Umayyad authorities of Córdoba (the capital) were under constant threat from Muslims who supported the Abbasid Caliphate.

conquests, virtually all of which were successful. For instance, Charlemagne pacified the Saxons in a war that lasted practically thirty years. The Saxons were a fierce, warlike Germanic tribe who were known by ancient Romans for their warcraft and zeal. Charlemagne successfully pacified the Saxons and managed to convert them to Christianity. Perhaps the most well-known war exploit of Charlemagne was his war against the Avars, who were Asiatic nomads who lived in modern-day Hungary. The campaign was particularly brutal. By 803, the Avars had been seriously weakened and had to accept Charlemagne as their supreme ruler.

Charlemagne also waged war on the Slavs in the north and south, further expanding his dominion. Thanks to all of these conquests, Charlemagne built an empire that spanned from Barcelona to modern-day Croatia and from modern-day Belgium all the way to Rome. This was an enormous empire, spanning across territories of modern-day Spain, France, Germany, Austria, Italy, Switzerland, Croatia, Hungary, Czechia, and Slovakia.

It was only natural for such a mighty individual to be coronated as the emperor of the Romans, Imperator Romanorum, in 800. Charlemagne ostensibly arrived in Rome to make peace between Pope Leo III and his adversaries. Humbled by Charlemagne's readiness to arrive and help, as well as by his conquests, Pope Leo III crowned Charlemagne and declared him to be Imperator Romanorum, a legitimate successor of Constantine VI, who ruled the Eastern Roman Empire and had been deposed by his mother, Irene, who proclaimed herself to be the empress. Pope Leo III didn't consider her a legitimate successor to the Roman heritage and found a better candidate in Charlemagne.

Francia at the accession of Charles Martel (714).

Although the coronation of Charlemagne legitimized his power in western and central Europe, it put him at odds with the Byzantine Empire, whose emperors considered themselves the only legitimate Roman emperors in Europe.[8] Western and eastern Europe were growing increasingly distant. Ultimately, the Byzantine Empire paid the highest price, as it was unable to do anything against the impending Muslim invasion. However, that would happen about six hundred years later. For now, we're still deep in the early medieval age, a time that was dominated by the Franks and Byzantines.

---

[8]Soon the political disunity would result in a religious split. In 1054, the Christian Church separated into two major currents, Catholic and Eastern Orthodox, an event today known as the Great Schism.

After Charlemagne

As is always the case with great empires, the Carolingian Empire was doomed right from the start. Overextension and internal troubles plagued the Carolingian Empire. We've seen that even prior to Charlemagne, there were internal conflicts for supremacy within the Carolingian dynasty. Rebels in practically all corners of the kingdom, as well as external enemies, were just waiting for the right opportunity to arrive.

Charlemagne died in 814, leaving his empire to Louis the Pious. He was the last ruler of the Carolingian Empire to rule alone. After Louis the Pious died in 840, his sons quickly reintroduced the old Frankish custom of dividing the kingdom between all legitimate successors, so the empire was divided once again in 843 in the Treaty of Verdun.

The empire was divided into three parts: *Francia occidentalis* (West Francia), ruled by Charles II; *Francia media* (Middle Francia), ruled by Lothair I; and *Francia orientalis* (East Francia), led by Louis II. East Francia took a majority of today's France. Middle Francia encompassed previous Frankish conquests in Italy and parts of Germany, France, and Switzerland. East Francia encompassed, roughly speaking, modern-day Germany and Austria.

The consequences of the Treaty of Verdun, in a way, are felt today, as this treaty gave basic contours to two European states: Germany and France.[9] There was a handful of other important treaties that followed and further partitioned the empire. The Treaty of Prüm in 855 saw Middle Francia partitioned into three new states: Italy, Lotharingia, and Provence. Perhaps the most important and far-reaching effect of this treaty was the formation of Lotharingia, which encompassed the Alsace and Lorraine regions, which became some of the major points of animosity between France and Germany in the centuries to come. In further treaties, namely the Treaty of Meerssen or Mersen (870) and the Treaty of Ribemont (880), the once mighty empire was further partitioned, with various provinces changing hands repeatedly.

There was, however, a brief period of unification under Charles the Fat from 881 to 888. The reunification of the empire and imperial coronation was rather haphazard. The Papal States, which had been

---

[9] Joranson, Einar. "The Dissolution of the Carolingian Fisc in the Ninth Century." (1936): 545-547.

under Frankish protection for years, were once again under threat from a regional warlord, and Pope John VIII sought help from Charles the Fat, who was the king of Frankish Italy and thus responsible for the security of the Papal States. Hoping for a revival of old power, the church coronated Charles the Fat, who, unfortunately, wasn't able to keep the empire unified.

Charles the Fat was unable to quench the rebellion rising in the eastern part of his empire. Arnulf of Carinthia, Charles's nephew, gathered a large army and defeated Charles the Fat, once again partitioning the empire.[10] This time, the division was much more long-lasting, with rare and relatively brief periods of reunification or mutual conquests. Arnulf of Carinthia ruled as the emperor until his death in 899.

In a similar vein, Louis the Blind, the adoptive son of Charles the Fat, tried to reunify the empire, but this was only a brief stint (901 to 905) that ended with him being blinded by the next big contender, Berengar I of Italy. This time, the interregnum period, the period between the death (or dethronement) of one ruler and the appointment of the new one, was even longer, with Berengar I of Italy becoming the emperor in 915.

Berengar I of Italy was in a good position to become the next emperor since he was the king of Italy and thus close to the pope. At the time (and more generally from the 9th to 11th century), Italy faced the so-called Saracen invasion in the south. Ancient Greeks and Romans sometimes referred, quite generally and indiscriminately, to Arabs as Saracens, and the name stuck for centuries. By the early 10th century, Arabs managed to gain a firm hold of Sicily, holding the island in its entirety and successfully repelling attacks from mainland Italy. Sicily served as a major Arab foothold in Italy, from where they could launch new invasions into mainland Italy and come dangerously close to Rome. A particular fortress built on the Garigliano River in central Italy was a thorn in the pope's side. Pope John X naturally didn't want Muslims on his doorstep and urged the noblemen of Christianized Europe to drive the Saracens away from Italy.

Summoned by Pope John X, Berengar sent his troops and put them under the command of Alberic I. Others sent troops too, like the

---

[10] Rosenberg, Harry. "Kingship and Politics in the Late Ninth Century: Charles the Fat and the End of the Carolingian Empire." The Historian 68, no. 3 (2006): 636-638.

Byzantine Empire and powerful princes, dukes, and counts of Italy. The Garigliano Saracen fortress would be the last Saracen stronghold to fall in the Christian forces' sweeping attack, doing so in 915. Sicily, however, was still firmly in Muslim hands, and it would stay that way for some time. Berengar had to pull his forces so they could assist in repelling the Magyars (Hungarians) who threatened the borders of the empire. The Magyars were able to penetrate far into western Europe, much like the Huns some four hundred years prior. The Hungarians threatened not only East and West Francia but also Italy and even the Córdoban Caliphate in Spain.

In the same year as the Battle of Garigliano, Berengar was crowned Holy Roman emperor, but this was merely an act of goodwill from the pope, who wanted to thank Berengar for lending a hand in the battle.[11] At the time, the Holy Roman Empire was merely an abstract concept, so it was an empty title. Berengar seemed to have been unable or unwilling to even attempt to reunite the Holy Roman Empire; truth be told, the Arab, Magyar, and Viking invaders made such a thing a very challenging task. Throughout his short-lived "reign" (from 915 to 924), Berengar also faced internal strife. He was attacked by his own grandson (also named Berengar) and had to face the animosity of Rudolph II of Upper Burgundy. The Battle of Firenzuola, which was fought in 923, sealed Berengar's fate; after this battle, Berengar of Italy was murdered in the city of Verona.

However, a new dynasty would enter the scene: the Ottonian dynasty.

---

[11] Merlo, Brian. "Pope John X and the End of the Formosan Dispute in Rome." PhD diss., Saint Louis University, 2018.

Chapter 2: Feudalism and the State of Early German Politics

Medieval States

The medieval period, for a variety of reasons, is referred to as the Dark Ages. This was a very challenging period in the development of human beings and marked a fairly abrupt end of the Roman culture, at least in western Europe. We'd like to emphasize that a lot of good things happened during the so-called Dark Ages. It's likely that without this period, which seems to be much hated by many people today, we wouldn't have the modern age we enjoy today.

However, unlike the Roman administration, medieval states were fairly undeveloped, and it would take centuries for states like France or Austria-Hungary to reach the level of state administration set by the ancient Romans. As the Roman Empire stepped down, numerous Germanic tribes stepped to the forefront. Once victorious, the Germanic people started forming their own states in Europe, as we've seen in the case of the Kingdom of the Franks.

These states were rather different than the Romans in more ways than one. For instance, they didn't rely on slave labor, though they did rely on something very similar: serfdom.[12] It's likely that various Germanic aristocratic families appeared long before the fall of Rome, fighting for supremacy against ethnically related tribes, as well as battling everyone

---

[12] Ganshof, François Louis. Feudalism. Vol. 34. University of Toronto Press, 1996.

else. These families owed their influence to their war prowess, strength, and wealth. They likely gave birth to some incredibly strong warriors who proved themselves on the battlefield countless times. To summarize, the ruling class among Germans was a class of influential warriors who were able to muster strong groups of soldiers that could outpower rival groups.

The serfs were much more numerous but less powerful. Their livelihood was based on raising agriculture and livestock, and they were subjugated to a small minority of aristocrats. The warriors/aristocrats tried to exert as much influence as they could upon the masses. In exchange for military protection, the serfs worked the land ("given" to them by their master) and gave a portion of their products to their master.

This is a very simple description of the feudal system. As we can see, the authority of feudal lords lay entirely in their military power, depending completely on their personal authority and ability to settle problems within their own dominion. Although a feudal lord wasn't exactly a god on earth, he would, in a way, exert the common law of the period, and his word was final. The feudal system gradually grew more complex, finally resulting in the formation of kingdoms with a single king overseeing a network of vassals on multiple levels. A typical medieval king (or emperor) was a powerful man, controlling vast areas and keeping other areas under his control, thanks to a network of vassals. He also drew his authority from the church. The church was instrumental in the establishment of the feudal system, as it allowed for the centralization of power by investing a single man with spiritual power to rule. Thus, the feudal king wasn't simply a powerful man; he was also perceived as being predetermined to rule by God himself.

A typical feudal king or emperor always had to strike a balance between the nobility and the church, as he was highly dependent on their readiness to support his claims to the throne. Feudal vassals were relatively independent, cushioned in their castles, and they were often very hard to control. They owed a formal allegiance to the king since he granted them their lands, and they were obliged to pay the ruler a certain sum and provide armies when the king waged war. At times, instead of supporting their king, a handful of feudal lords teamed up against the king to increase their own influence. The king, in turn, would muster the forces of his true allies and pacify the rebels. The medieval age also saw endless conflicts between vassals themselves. For instance, the lowest vassal in the network, usually a local warlord of sorts, would attack his closest neighbor over some insignificant feud or territorial dispute.

If one refers to the medieval age as the "Dark Ages," it should be because of the inherent instability of the feudal system. Violence, war, and plunder were exceedingly common; in fact, they were too common for anything other than a very slow civilizational progress. Towns in Italy, which were among the most developed in Europe and the heralds of the Renaissance, were destroyed countless times in the medieval age. For centuries, German rulers descended south to pacify rebellious Italian towns and take the imperial crown. However, in Germany (and elsewhere in Europe), periods of peace and stability were separated by long years of internal strife, with high-ranking nobles rebelling against the emperor and against each other. Occasionally, a powerful leader emerged who was able to balance the demands of the nobility, the church, and the caste that often gets forgotten in discussions about the medieval age, the commoners, through the use of force and careful diplomacy. However, much more often, rulers didn't want or were unable to strike this balance, leading to chaos. Instability would often last for years without respite. Indeed, the feudal system brought forth the social state referred to by Thomas Hobbes as the "natural condition of mankind," in which only pure physical force determines one's outcome in life.

Keeping this in mind, it isn't surprising that it was exceedingly hard for medieval states, such as the Holy Roman Empire, to achieve any degree of centralization. There were many families vying for supremacy. One would prevail over another thanks to its military supremacy, but then another family would rise up and take everything by force. However, there was at least some kind of structure to the relationships between feudal lords, which was finally formalized in the Golden Bull of 1356.

It was customary among the most powerful Germans to periodically meet and choose the first amongst themselves. The Golden Bull defined the seven electors who would meet to choose the new king of the Romans (who would inevitably become the Holy Roman emperor once the pope approved): the duke of Saxony, the count palatine of Rhine, the margrave of Brandenburg, and the king of Bohemia. Three electors were ecclesiastical officials, the archbishops of Mainz, Cologne, and Trier. For centuries, Germans elected their king in a similar fashion, and they applied the same principle to the election of the new king of the

Romans (Holy Roman emperor). More electors would be added as time went on, though the Habsburgs, in the end, managed to establish themselves as supreme rulers, nullifying the process of imperial elections completely.

The Golden Bull was the culmination of a long process that allowed Germans to elect the strongest feudal lord amongst themselves. It was a counterweight to the often brutal nature of relationships between families, tribes, and regions of Germany. Keeping this in mind, let's continue with our story and move toward our new stop, the Ottonian dynasty.

Chapter 3: The Ottonian Dynasty

The Rise of the Ottonian Dynasty: Setting the Stage for a New Era

After the transitory reunification under Charles the Fat, the Frankish-Carolingian Empire finally broke down under the burden of civil wars. In a sense, two major blocs formed, French and German, and they constantly vied for supremacy in the region.

The next crucial characters in our story come from the Ottonian line.[13] They were Germans but not Franks, and they were the first non-Frankish dynasty to take over the throne of the Holy Roman Empire. This dynasty was started by a regional warlord, Liudolf of Saxony, in the 9th century. The Ottonians played a major role in the history of the Holy Roman Empire. Liudolf's younger son, known as Otto the Illustrious, became the head of Saxony in 880, succeeding Bruno, his older brother, who died in combat fighting against the Vikings. It's likely that Otto the Illustrious was less crude in comparison to his brother, which earned him the nickname "Illustrious," although not much is known about his personal characteristics that earned him the nickname.

Henry the Fowler succeeded Otto the Illustrious when the latter died in 912. Initially the duke of Saxony, Henry the Fowler became king of East Francia in 919, a title he received from Conrad I. Soon enough, Henry also received the Holy Lance from Rudolph II, King of

---

[13] MacLean, Simon. "History and Politics in Late Carolingian and Ottonian Europe: The Chronicle of Regino of Prüm and Adalbert of Magdeburg." In History and Politics in Late Carolingian and Ottonian Europe. Manchester University Press, 2013.

Burgundy and Italy, around 922.[14] This version of the alleged Holy Lance is said to have been the lance once used by the mighty Emperor Constantine; its holiness was amplified since it supposedly encased the nails used to crucify Christ.

The Holy Lance wasn't simply a prestigious relic exuding mystical religious sentiments and symbolic power; it was also a political tool. Historians argue that the transfer of the Holy Lance in the 10th century was a political gesture, a finalization of a political pact. The exchange of a precious relic sealed deals between people who had been at war with each other. As we've seen and as we'll see, it wasn't unusual for the various kings, dukes, counts, and warlords of the ex-Carolingian Empire to wage war against one another. The predecessors of Rudolph II and Henry the Fowler are great examples of this precarious political situation. The transfer of the Holy Lance from Rudolph II to Henry the Fowler must have held a symbolic meaning of a peace treaty.

It's likely that Henry owes his nickname to his great love for hunting and bird-hunting since "fowler" essentially means "individual who hunts wildfowl." According to legend, Henry was so consumed by hunting that the news of him becoming a king reached him while he was hunting for birds (hence his nickname).

Henry the Fowler was perhaps more expansion-minded than his father. Even before becoming a king, Henry fought for Thuringia. After becoming a king, he set his eyes on Lotharingia, Bohemia, Schleswig, the northern Alps, and other regions. He also defended his territory from the Magyars (Hungarians), who were a major invading force in eastern and central Europe at the time. The Magyars were probably the most problematic for Henry. For a period, the Kingdom of Germany was even forced to pay annual tribute to the Magyars, who were able to inflict defeats upon Henry's forces. Eventually, however, Henry was able to strengthen his army (especially his heavy cavalry), build new fortifications, and repulse the Magyars once and for all.

---

[14]HAUFF, Andrea. The Kingdom of Upper Burgundy and the East Frankish Kingdom at the Beginning of the 10th Century. *History Compass*, 2017, 15.8: e12396.

Painting by Hermann Vogel (1854–1921), showing the legend of Henry receiving the news of his election.

One of the strongest points of Henry's army and the Holy Roman Empire was most certainly the heavy cavalry. The heavy cavalry was made up of knights, skilled warriors who often wore heavy armor. They were a formidable force throughout the Middle Ages. It wasn't until cannons were introduced on a wider scale to European warfare that heavy cavalry became a thing of the past. During the reigns of Henry the Fowler and his immediate successors, the heavy cavalry was one of the most important military formations, as they were able to turn the tide of the battle and inflict heavy damage upon infantry and archers. This was why the people who constituted the heavy cavalry units were very important and much respected by their fellow countrymen and especially by their rulers.

We don't know for sure whether these early knights were noblemen from the start and thus able to procure the best equipment or whether they were simply skilled fighters who earned respect due to their merit. It's likely there was a mixture of both. In any case, knights quickly became noblemen and were instrumental in the feudal system of the Middle Ages.[15]

It is difficult to state how important the heavy cavalry was for the rise of both the Carolingians and the Holy Roman Empire. The heavy cavalry was the elite unit, the most modern and advanced for its age, much like tank divisions in the Second World War or drones in modern warfare.

Henry the Fowler, much like his predecessors and his successors, made good use of the heavy cavalry that was available to him. Moreover, he wasn't as interested in centralizing power and was happy to have worthy and honorable feudal lords in various regions he controlled. Those lords all had their own heavy cavalry units that could be called up to service when necessary. Feudal lords enjoyed a sort of autonomy and had absolute power within their fiefs, but they were ultimately subordinate to the king (or emperor). So, in times of war, they were tasked with levying armies in their respective provinces.

The Golden Age under the Ottonians

Henry the Fowler died in 936 and was succeeded by his son, Otto the Great, who was only around twenty-four at the time. He eventually became the first true Holy Roman emperor. Otto the Great, much like his father, worked hard to unify the Germans into a single nation. Unlike Henry, Otto the Great was more interested in centralizing power in the style of the Carolingian monarchs, which gave rise to internal strife that was quickly quenched by Otto.

Otto wanted to confirm the connection between the Carolingians and himself. He strove for that imperial allure that surrounded Charlemagne. That was why he wore a traditional Frankish robe for his coronation in 936.

---

[15]BACHRACH, David Stewart. Milites and Warfare in Pre-Crusade Germany. *War in History*, 2015, 22.3: 298-343.

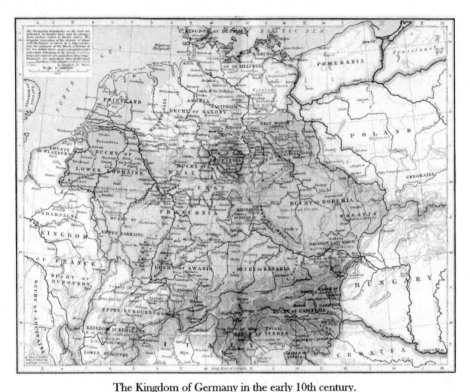

The Kingdom of Germany in the early 10th century.
https://commons.wikimedia.org/w/index.php?curid=2009655

More importantly, Otto the Great laid the foundations of an intricate administration that would help disseminate royal power across the vast lands of the Holy Roman Empire.[16] Otto the Great, unlike, say, Louis the Blind or Berengar I of Italy, would hold his ground for many years and had a clear vision when it came to uniting the Holy Roman Empire. Otto the Great, as king of East Francia, slowly but surely weakened internal and external enemies. He formally became the Holy Roman emperor in 962.

[16]BACHRACH, David. Exercise of royal power in early medieval Europe: the case of Otto the Great 936–73. *Early Medieval Europe*, 2009, 17.4: 389-419.

Crown of the Holy Roman emperor.

Before becoming emperor, Otto the Great faced a civil war in 938 and again in 953. He fought numerous enemies, such as Henry (his younger brother), Liudolf (his son), and the dukes of Franconia, Lotharingia, and Swabia. In 938, there was a local conflict in Saxony between Lord Bruning and Duke Eberhard of Franconia. Bruning wouldn't respond to Eberhard's orders. So, Eberhard violently took Bruning's castle and killed all the inhabitants. Otto reprimanded Eberhard for this kind of behavior. Besides paying a large fine, Eberhard's men were publicly shamed and ordered to carry the carcasses of dogs in public.

This must have been outrageous to Eberhard, and he decided to start open hostilities with Otto. He sided with Thankmar, Otto's half-brother, and some other local lords. The rebellion was quickly quenched by Otto. Thankmar, in turn, was captured and executed in the Church of St. Peter in Eresburg.[17] Other conspirators, chiefly Eberhard, ostensibly proclaimed their submission to Otto, but in reality, they were planning a new rebellion.

Another conflict broke out in 939. Once again, Eberhard was in the midst of it. This time, Eberhard convinced Henry, who was the king of West Francia and Otto's younger brother, and they declared war on Otto. Others jumped onto the merry war bandwagon, like Gilbert, Duke of Lorraine. The decisive battle was fought near Andernach in 939, and Otto's forces crushed the enemy. Gilbert and Eberhard were both killed, with the former drowning in the Rhine and the latter being killed in action.[18] Otto's brother Henry was spared, and the brothers reconciled by 940 due to their mother's mediation.

However, Henry wasn't satisfied with his new dukedom of Lorraine. He wanted the whole cake for himself, so he tried to defeat Otto through different means: assassination. The plot was discovered, and all the conspirators were swiftly arrested. Otto eventually pardoned the conspirators, though only after they formally and publicly sought penance for their crimes, in 941.

Otto the Great didn't kill his brother. He sought reconciliation again and tried to find a peaceful solution. This time, he was successful. Henry couldn't complain about receiving the dukedom of Bavaria around 948.[19]

Otto the Great was a very active ruler and even traveled throughout his vast lands. It's likely he was rather tall and physically imposing, as well as charismatic and bold. He would stay in major cities for around a week, where he would talk to locals, convincing them that he was "the chosen one." He must have been a good negotiator and communicator because he was able to make peace between noblemen who were often hostile to each other.

---

[17] It is possible that Otto the Great ordered this execution.
[18] BACHRACH, David S. Early Ottonian Warfare: The Perspective from Corvey. *Journal of Military History*, 2011, 75.2.
[19] WILSON, Joseph. Holy Anointment and Realpolitik in the Age of Otto I. 2015.

As we've seen in the cases of Eberhard and Henry, Otto the Great tried hard to avoid capital punishment. This wasn't simply an act of royal benevolence; it was also a very pragmatic move. Back in the day, blood feuds were still a tradition and something held in high esteem. If someone from your family was murdered, your task (provided you were a mature male) was to find and kill the murderer of your family member. Needless to say, blood feuds have a tendency to never end because someone always seeks revenge.

In other words, Otto was a wise ruler who knew how to disseminate his royal prestige across his kingdom. It isn't surprising that he was able to levy enormous armies that could stop the Magyar invaders. In 955, a decisive battle between the Magyars and Otto the Great's forces occurred. It was called the Battle of Lechfeld.

Similar to the Huns who came before them, the Magyars deployed thousands of agile horse archers who could cover large distances and inflict chaos across Europe. Before the Battle of Lechfeld, the Magyars invaded some lands in Bavaria and besieged Augsburg (the city is built around the Lech River, hence the name of the battle). Otto the Great was able to muster around eight thousand heavy cavalrymen, who rushed to relieve Augsburg.

The Magyars wanted to defeat Otto in an open battle and finally met Otto's army close to Augsburg. The Magyars' light cavalry and horse archers were no match for Otto's heavy cavalry, and the Magyars were soon forced to retreat. The Magyars also made some bad decisions. After successfully routing the Bohemian legion, they stopped to plunder the legion's cargo and provisions, which provided a great opportunity for the Germans to catch them off guard. One can only try to imagine the dread of being caught off guard by a heavy cavalry charge.

The bulk of Otto's forces then directly faced the Magyars, drawing them into close combat, which was somewhat more favorable for the Germans since they had better armor. With heavy casualties on both sides, the Magyars started to retreat in an orderly fashion, and Otto decided to call it a day. He didn't want to pursue the Magyars, probably because he knew that their cavalry was more agile and able to fire back during the retreat. Instead, Otto retreated to Augsburg and ordered all roads and river crossings in the region to be closed to impede further Magyar retreats. Over the next few days, the Magyars became encircled, making their retreat to eastern Europe made impossible. They were then hunted down and executed, one by one.

This was an illustrious victory, and it transformed Otto into an emperor, though Otto would have to wait a bit longer to be formally crowned as the Holy Roman emperor.

Even though Otto the Great was constantly on the move, he managed to lay the foundations for an efficient administration. By his time, the state had access to archives regarding property and lands of the aristocracy. We know this because Otto sometimes confiscated lands from certain counts, dukes, and lords, meaning he knew which lands to confiscate. He redistributed the lands to more docile members of the noblesse. For instance, after Count Guntram fell out of grace in 952, the court knew exactly what Guntram owned. He was quickly stripped of all his earthly belongings.

Otto depicted on a coin.
https://commons.wikimedia.org/w/index.php?curid=1668262

Next, like some of his predecessors, namely Charlemagne and Louis the Pious, Otto the Great possessed a mobile library/archive, which was always available to him for consultation even when on the road.

Careful archiving (before and during the reign of Otto the Great) allowed for requisitions of land. Estates were taken away from disobedient members of the aristocracy, but Otto sometimes had designs and plans that necessitated land requisitioning from the church, which was an unpleasant but necessary practice. For instance, in 940, Otto the Great (at the time still just a king) authorized the return of Moosburg Monastery to its original owner (the Freising family), mentioning machinations and illegal practices as the primary means through which the church obtained the monastery in the first place.[20] There's a myriad of other similar court proceedings in which Otto was embroiled, and these stand as a testament to some of the more tedious but equally important activities of a medieval ruler.

Otto the Great managed to assert himself as a powerful king by defeating the Magyars in 955, even being hailed as *imperator* and *pater patriae* by his own troops after the Battle of Lechfeld, a custom that stems back to the times of ancient Rome. But there were still a few things to be done before he became an emperor.

Prior to defeating the Magyars, Otto the Great married Adelaide in 951. She had been the queen of Italy, so the marriage could be seen as an attempt to ease Otto's way to the Italian throne, which, in turn, would have allowed him to be crowned as the Holy Roman emperor.

Otto was careful about his relationship with the church. He managed to install relatives in high church offices, such as his brother Bruno, who became the archbishop of Cologne in 953. William, Otto's illegitimate son, became the archbishop of Meinz, and other high church officials were also all "Otto's men." Otto tried to present himself as the "holy anointed one," someone who was chosen by God to rule.

Otto managed to assert his position as the protector of the church when Berengar II, King of Italy, started becoming more rebellious. He attempted to take some territories he had been deprived of earlier by Otto. Berengar II also menaced the Papal States themselves, and Pope John XII's appeal ultimately pulled Otto into Italy. The trade-off was rather clear: the pope got back his security, while Otto became the Holy Roman emperor.

Otto levied his forces and entered Italy in 961. By 962, he was able to enter Italy and reach Rome. January 31st, 962, was the day Pope John XII anointed Otto as the emperor of the Holy Roman Empire in St.

---

[20] BACHRACH, David S. Early Ottonian Warfare: The Perspective from Corvey. *Journal of Military History*, 2011, 75.2.

Peter's Basilica. Early sources are surprisingly quiet about the details of the coronation, especially in comparison to Otto's previous coronation as the king of Germany in Aachen in 936.[21]

Lacking a contemporary description of the 962 coronation, let's turn briefly to the Aachen coronation. Otto was first lauded outside of the Aachen chapel by the most illustrious Franks and Saxons. This was repeated in the chapel itself, after which Otto was presented with the royal insignia. He was then anointed by the clergy, crowned, and finally allowed to sit on his throne in the Aachen Cathedral.

It's possible that the 962 coronation followed a similar pattern. Moreover, the relative silence of contemporary sources with respect to the coronation might be indicative of the future Investiture Controversy. Namely, why would Otto the Great need to accept his imperial crown from a pope? Isn't a Holy Roman emperor mightier than all the clergy combined? As far as Otto and the Germans were concerned, he had already been the emperor for about seven years in 962; he had been emperor since the Battle of Lechfeld in 955. The fact that the pope finally decided to proclaim Otto as emperor was, for all intents and purposes, insignificant.

It was obvious that Otto had the upper hand and more power in comparison to the pope. Otto also finally quenched Berengar's rebellion in 963, only doing so after receiving the imperial crown. That Pope John XII was, in a way, coerced into accepting Otto as the Holy Roman emperor might be supported by the fact that soon after the coronation, he attempted to weaken Otto's position and was subsequently deposed.[22] It is interesting that Pope John XII is depicted as a "monster" and "traitor" by some of the early chroniclers of Otto's reign.[23] The pope was accused of siding with Berengar's son, Adalbert. He was also reprimanded for his alleged sexual exploits, as well as for the wretched state of Rome's numerous churches. Otto the Great organized a large council in Rome in St. Peter's Basilica, which was attended by numerous archbishops, bishops, and members of the clergy and the Roman elite.

[21]Robbie, Steven. "Can Silence Speak Volumes? Widukind's Res Gestae Saxonicae and the Coronation of Otto I Reconsidered." Early Medieval Europe 20, no. 3 (2012): 333-362.
[22]Poole, Reginald L. "The Names and Numbers of Medieval Popes." The English Historical Review 32, no. 128 (1917): 465-478.
[23]Grabowski, Antoni. "Liudprand of Cremona's papa monstrum: The Image of Pope John XII in the Historia Ottonis." Early Medieval Europe 23, no. 1 (2015): 67-92.

This council quickly deposed Pope John XII in 963.

It is interesting how accusations against Pope John XII merged together to depict a person of wretched morale. He was not only a traitor but also a sexually promiscuous person. For instance, Pope John XII allegedly raped women in churches, had incestuous relations with his aunt, and held a brothel. Truth be told, in the 10th century, celibacy wasn't a necessary prerequisite for the Roman clergy. In fact, some priests were even married, and even more of them were widely known to be sexually active.[24] However, the crimes leveled against John XII were outrageous even in the somewhat lenient atmosphere of 10th-century Rome.

John XII never responded to these accusations; he ran away from Rome when he heard about the council being organized to depose him. The new pope was Leo VIII (chosen by Otto the Great), who must have had an even worse reputation because John XII managed to get back to Rome in 964 and cause Leo's own deposal with the help of the populace of Rome. Otto had disassembled his army and left Rome soon after deposing John XII. Upon hearing about the return of the ghastly John XII, Otto started planning a siege of Rome, but John's death was faster. In May 964, Pope John XII died, and Benedict V became the new pope, as he was desired by the Romans. Benedict V wasn't really Otto's favorite, so he, too, was exiled, and Leo VIII was brought back as the head of the church.

This short episode is one of numerous examples from the turbulent history of the Roman Church. As we can see, the Roman Church had its own scandals and affairs more than one thousand years ago. For now, though, let's focus on the end of Otto's reign and then quickly go through the reigns of his successors.

By 966, and after several more hiccups in Italy, Otto had decided to make Rome his permanent residence. Otto wanted to gradually subjugate the whole of Italy and once and for all crush the rebellion that had been fomenting in Italy for quite some time. Once again, Otto didn't allow for free elections of the new pope. After Leo VIII died in 965, another favorite of Otto became the new pope: John XIII. Pope John XIII continued what some authors call "pornocracy" in Rome, or at least that's how it appeared to be to the members of the Roman nobility.

---

[24]Ibid. p. 76

(Pornocracy is when morally decadent, sexually promiscuous, and debauched individuals are allowed to govern.)[25] Like his predecessor, Leo VIII, John XIII was ousted from Rome and even held in captivity. And once again, Otto had to return to Italy with a large army. This time, he was more determined than ever to crush those who dared to bring John's and his own authority into question.[26]

John XIII ordered a ruthless punishment of one of the rebellion's instigators, Peter, the Prefect of Rome, whose forces were instrumental in capturing and ousting John from Rome. Peter went through a whole ordeal of public shaming. First, he was left to hang from the statue of Marcus Aurelius. Then, he was stripped naked and placed on a donkey backward. Finally, he was adorned with feathers and taken for a ride through the whole city.

One of Otto the Great's final important political actions was his rapprochement with the Byzantine Empire. The conflict between the Holy Roman Empire and the Byzantine Empire was twofold. Both empires believed southern Italy was their exclusive dominion, and both empires wanted to be the sole successors of the great Roman Empire. Otto the Great was able to find a compromise. The Byzantines agreed to recognize him as the Holy Roman emperor without seriously undermining their own authority, and Otto the Great agreed to leave southern Italy (Apulia and Calabria) to the Byzantines. In addition, Emperor John I Tzimiskes agreed to have his niece Theophano (also spelled Theophanu) married to Otto's son, Otto II, with the marriage being completed in 972.[27] For a brief period, the animosities between the East and West subsided, and the two empires were able to focus on other problems.

Otto the Great returned to Germany, where he celebrated Easter in 973. He died shortly after at the age of sixty. His youngest son, Otto II, who was seventeen at the time, rose to the imperial throne. Otto's older sons had all died, which made the youngest son the heir apparent.

---

[25]Brook, Lindsay. "Popes and Pornocrats: Rome in the Early Middle Ages." Foundations 1, no. 1 (2003): 5-21.

[26]Roach, Levi. "The Ottonians and Italy." German History 36, no. 3 (2018): 349-364.

[27]Osborne, John. "The Dower Charter of Otto II and Theophanu, and the Roman Scriptorium at Santi Apostoli." Papers of the British School at Rome 89 (2021): 137-157.

Decline and Transition

Otto II (Otto the Red) had the intention of furthering his father's plans for the Holy Roman Empire, though he wasn't able to do much. He died at the age of twenty-eight in 983, probably due to malaria, which was present in Europe at the time, especially in Italy, where Otto II died. Throughout the ten years of his reign, he managed to keep the Holy Roman Empire united, crushing rebellions and nurturing hopes of expanding his dominion into southern Italy. However, these hopes were ended by his premature death, which also plunged the precarious Holy Roman Empire into a state of chaos.[28] The son of Otto II, Otto III, was only three at the time, which, needless to say, sparked a succession crisis. A rift between Otto III's caregivers (his mother, Theophano, and his grandmother, Adelaide) and Henry II, Duke of Bavaria, appeared. Duke Henry II ("the Quarrelsome") was closely related to the imperial family; his father was Otto the Great's younger brother.

Initially, it looked as if Henry the Quarrelsome would take over the custody of Otto III because he was the first one to reach the young emperor after his father's death. Adelaide and Theophano were still in Italy when Henry reached young Otto III in Aachen. From 983 to 984, Henry, in a way, was hailed as a king throughout Germany. With the two empresses returning to Germany and garnering support from the nobility, Henry was forced to return Otto III to his mother and grandmother. In return, Henry was pardoned for treason.[29]

Otto III remained under the custody of his mother and grandmother until 994, when he turned fourteen. The two empresses managed to keep the Holy Roman Empire together, at least ostensibly, leaving it to the young Otto III, who was supposed to silence the nobility that, in the absence of a firm ruler, started straying away from the unity Otto the Great had been able to achieve.

The young emperor suffered the same faith as his father. He died in 1002 in Italy, presumably from malaria. And like his father, Otto III was supposed to be married to a Byzantine princess. Princess Zoe Porphyrogenita, daughter of Emperor Constantine VIII, was on her way

---

[28]Welton, Megan, and Sarah Greer. "Establishing Just Rule: The Diplomatic Negotiations of the Dominae Imperiales in the Ottonian Succession Crisis of 983–985." Frühmittelalterliche Studien 55, no. 1 (2021): 315-342.
[29]Ibid.

to Italy to marry Otto III, but his death was quicker. After his death, a new succession crisis emerged, which ended with the election of Henry the Exuberant, son of Henry II the Quarrelsome.

Henry II ("the Exuberant") formally became the emperor in 1014 when he was crowned by Pope Benedict VIII. Like his predecessor, Otto III, Henry II didn't have children, which produced another succession crisis when he died in 1024. This opened up space for the Salians to come onto the scene. A highly religious emperor, Henry the Exuberant was the only medieval German ruler canonized by the church; his wife was also canonized.

But for all his devout religiousness, Henry II was one of the sources of the Investiture Crisis (or Investiture Controversy), which will be discussed in the next chapter. Namely, Henry II strengthened the imperial grip of the church, making sure that everyone in the empire knew-that the church was not only the responsibility of the ecclesiastical personnel (priests, bishops, archbishops, the pope, etc.) but also the responsibility of the Holy Roman Empire.[30] For instance, Henry II wanted to legalize the empire's right to intervene in church matters, such as choice of pope or archbishops, a practice that had already been in use for some time. Needless to say, the pope and the church didn't agree with this stance. However, during the reign of Henry II, possibly thanks to his charisma, animosities were put aside, only to resurface soon after during the reign of the Salians.

[30]ZELLER, Jules. L'empire germanique et l'Eglise au Moyen-Age: les Henri. Didier, 1876.

Chapter 4: Salian Rule and the Investiture Crisis

Prelude to the Investiture Crisis

As was customary among the Germans, after the ruler died without an heir apparent, elections were held among the nobility to choose the new ruler. Conrad II, whose great-grandmother Liutgarde was the daughter of Otto the Great, was chosen as the new German king thanks to his rich life experience and stable family life (Conrad II had a son who could inherit the throne).

The Ottonians had a somewhat ambiguous relationship with the church. Saint Henry (Henry II), the last Ottonian emperor, is a perfect example of this relationship. On the one hand, he was a highly religious man and contributed to the establishment and dissemination of the church hierarchy across the Holy Roman Empire. When the Salians marched onto the scene, the church had already become a powerful tool and was on equal terms with the secular nobility and feudal lords. The church, in a way, ensured the transition between rulers and dynasties. However, the first Salian German king, Conrad II, who had been elected by a council of nobles and religious authorities, still had some issues with rebels in Germany and Italy. After silencing the dissenting voices in Germany, he turned toward Italy, where he was crowned as the Holy Roman emperor in St. Peter's Basilica in 1027.

To understand the conflict between the Salians and the Roman Church, we first have to understand how the church became such a crucial instrument in the hands of the Ottonians, especially Henry II. Church officials, priests, bishops, and archbishops became, in a way, more important than feudal lords. They were responsible not only for otherworldly matters but also for the arrangement of worldly matters. For instance, in Lorsch Abbey, there was a monastery, and the church officials there were responsible for gathering a force of ten thousand men by Henry II.[31] There was a sort of balance between the church's own powers (conferred to them by the emperor) and its submission to the emperor.

However, when the Salians came to power, this balance was brought into question. Conrad II and his successors relied more on the secular nobility to ensure the submission of vast areas of the Holy Roman Empire. The Salians were a very old family; they were able to track their ancestry way back to the early days of the first Frankish states (even before the Carolingians came to power).[32] They owed their ascent to power to this illustrious heritage.

It is interesting, though, that the first Salian ruler, Conrad II, was mostly illiterate, much like other German medieval leaders who would come after him. However, Conrad's incomplete grasp of reading and writing didn't really make him unable to rule. In any case, medieval leaders owed their authority to their war prowess and the amount of force they could muster; their education was secondary.

Conrad II inherited a very peculiar empire. In spite of carrying the name of the ancient Roman Empire, the Holy Roman Empire had a much weaker administration (it was virtually nonexistent, in fact) in comparison to the Roman Empire. Although the Ottonians were fond of warfare, they tried to usher in at least some sort of administration with the help of the church, which would become, in a way, the right hand of the imperial family. But for all intents and purposes, the Holy Roman Empire was just an idea, a sort of prestige that numerous rulers tried to attain without really managing to establish a permanent government over the vast areas they allegedly possessed. This was why each ruler in the Ottonian dynasty literally had to reconquer some of "his" lands immediately after rising to power. When the Ottonians pacified Italy, problems would break out elsewhere.

[31]Zeller, Jules. L'empire germanique et l'Eglise au Moyen-Age: les Henri. Vol. 3. Didier, 1876.
[32]Ibid.

It was up to the Salians to attempt to solve this big issue of governing such a vast territory. Conrad II faced all the usual troubles. As soon as he took over the title of king of the Germans, he faced rebellious nobles, such as Rudolf III, King of Burgundy; Ernest II, Duke of Swabia; and Odo, Count of Champagne. They felt they were only subordinate to the Ottonians, not to the newly elected Salian dynasty. As we will see, the idea of subordination was largely personal. It's not that a nation was a part of a larger nation or state; it's just that two leaders agreed on something between them. The concept of power was personal and also concrete, as it could be expressed through the very real force a ruler could exert.

Conrad II reaffirmed the heredity of singular fiefs, making it harder for them to be alienated from the families that traditionally governed them. By doing this, he cast light on the perennial rift between worldly and spiritual powers.

Conrad II faced considerable resistance in Italy. The Roman Church planned to proclaim Prince Guillaume (William) of Aquitaine as emperor. He refused, knowing he would only be a pawn in the game of chess played by Italian popes, archbishops, and bishops. In 1026, Conrad II arrived in Italy with a fairly large army, making sure everyone in Italy knew what could happen if they decided to disobey him. Conrad's arrival and stay in Italy sometimes seemed more like a brutal invasion than a visit to one of the parts of his vast empire. Some towns dared not open their doors to the German king, and they paid dearly for their disobedience. The town of Pavia was spared, but its routes and vineyards weren't. Ravenna suffered even more. Conrad II's soldiers were let in, but scuffles between them and confused inhabitants started to break out. The gates of Ravenna were then closed, and those soldiers who made their way into the city were chased through the streets and slaughtered. Upon hearing of this, Conrad II let his soldiers enter the city in order to avenge their fallen brethren.[33]

This sort of scenario was more a rule than an exception for the German conquests in Italy. Each German king (to-be-emperor or already the Holy Roman emperor) arrived with a large army. As the proverb goes, "A large army is always disorderly." A large army has to be fed, clothed, and sheltered, and over time, this becomes an incredible

---

[33]Ibid. p. 39

burden for the nation that receives the army. Moreover, Italian towns, culturally speaking, were much more advanced than towns in Germany. The people were somewhat less crude and warlike than the Germans. People in Italy didn't really like seeing endless masses of German warriors ravaging their fields and towns. This was the deeper reason why each German king had to essentially reconquer Italy in order to be proclaimed the Holy Roman emperor.

Conrad II reached Rome by March 1027. The pope at the time was John XIX, who wasn't really on friendly terms with Conrad II. The coronation didn't go well. While the ceremony was still being performed, a fight broke out between the Germans and the Romans. A German soldier allegedly tried to steal some leather from a Roman. In the scuffle that broke out, an aristocrat from Sweden was killed. He was then brutally avenged by the German soldiers. Those who participated in the combat were punished the following day, with the punishment being accomplished with the very weapons they used to hurt others the day before.

Conrad II stayed in Italy for almost two years. While he was busy pacifying Italy, nobles in Germany, profiting from the absence of their emperor, started to rebel. Ernest, Count of Swabia, was the most important figure in this new rebellion, although he was joined by many others. The main reason for this rebellion was the conflict between the old nobility and the new church elite. The high nobles felt their power was being diluted while the church became ever more powerful.

But here, Conrad's clairvoyance came to the forefront. Earlier, he demanded an oath, not only from the high nobles but also from the lower nobles who were traditionally directly responsible to dukes and counts but not necessarily to the emperor. Now, they all had a feeling of direct obedience to the emperor, so they would regularly abandon their dukes and counts when they rebelled against Conrad II.

After quenching this rebellion, Conrad appointed his oldest son as his heir apparent. He didn't leave anything to chance. All the other sons of Conrad were eventually sent to monasteries, where they could do little to endanger the authority of their oldest brother. This nicely shows the position of the church during Conrad II's reign. The church was an instrument of power and was ultimately subordinate to the emperor.

While Conrad II took great care to be on good terms with the low nobility, ensuring the hereditary status of their lands, he did the exact opposite with the high nobility. Whenever he could, Conrad II would take away the hereditary status of important dukedoms and feuds so that he could gradually, through strategic marriages, bring more and more land into his own family. He started to remove all the intermediaries between the lower nobility and himself, eradicating the vain ambition of dukes, counts, and princes. The lower nobility, however, was fragmented, as it was fairly hard for them to join their strengths and come to terms: there were simply too many of them. On the other hand, a few dukes and counts could easily meet and decide whether they wanted to rebel or not. In a way, this was a start, however timid and slow, of the formation of the modern German identity. The "small" German nations of Swabia and Bavaria were stripped of their leaders and slowly began melting into one universal German identity.

But at the same time, this was the root of the Investiture Crisis. Conrad II weakened the position of the church and, in a way, functioned like a pagan leader who was only on good terms with the church as long as it served his interests. He dealt with ecclesiastical matters as long as he could draw profit and gain something for himself and his family. Everything else (perhaps the more spiritual and idealistic things admired by Henry II) was of secondary importance.

The ruling German dynasty supported whoever would ensure the church's subservience. Conrad II even allowed for the ascension of a very young man to the papacy, who owed this ascent to his father's bribery.[34] In 1032, Benedict IX was proclaimed the new pope. It's not certain just how old he was at the time, but according to some sources, he might have been as young as twelve. Most historians believe he was around twenty years of age, which still makes him the youngest person to ever sit in St. Peter's chair. He is also the only pope to serve more than once. Benedict's age and way of attaining the papacy would have been disgraceful for the more pious Henry II, but for the pragmatic Conrad II, this wasn't an issue at all.

It isn't surprising that rebellion started to foment in Italy as early as 1035. A number of nobles, vassals, and rich townspeople united in northern Italy and rebelled against Archbishop Heribert, who was basically the personification of imperial power in Italy. By 1036, Conrad II had reached Italy with a large army to personally quench this

---

[34]Ibid.

37

rebellion. He tried to introduce similar changes to the ones he already applied in Germany. Namely, Conrad II tried to reduce the powers of the high nobility by demanding personal subservience from the lesser nobles.

During the last few years of his life, Conrad II spent most of his time in Italy, trying to once and for all destroy any power that dared question his own. In 1039, he returned to Germany, but he fell ill and soon died. He laid the foundations for a different sort of Holy Roman Empire, one that was proud of its terrestrial power and endlessly thirsty to enlarge itself. Henry III logically continued the work started by Conrad II.

Henry III ("the Dark") was much better educated than his father. His nickname comes from his dark beard, which might have been fairly unusual in 11th-century Germany. He was described as pious, humble, beautiful, courageous, and a lover of peace.[35] However, being a lover of peace had a different meaning in the medieval age, a time when war was more of a standard part of life. Henry III engaged in numerous wars across Europe; it was as if he was driven by an irresistible compulsion. First came Bohemian Prince Bretislav, who conquered Poland, which had fallen into a sort of anarchy and experienced a revival of pagan traditions. Bretislav, a major defender of Christianity, invaded Poland, possibly with the pretext of bringing back much-needed order and the Christian religion. Henry III didn't really like this territorial expansion by Bretislav, and he wanted Bretislav to retreat from Poland, to which the latter simply said no. In 1040, there was an attempted conquest of Bohemia, which was ultimately unsuccessful since the invading German forces were constantly ambushed from the thick Polish forests. The next year, Henry returned with an even larger army, this time attacking Bretislav's center of power, Prague.

Next came Hungary, which had also been recently Christianized. King Stephen, Hungary's first Christian king, left a highly educated and civilized son, Peter, to rule the country. However, Peter was unable to placate the still very much uncivilized Hungarians and was ousted by Samuel Aba, a prominent Hungarian noble. Samuel went on to destroy some German settlements, which attracted Henry's attention. Henry's first Hungarian expedition in 1042 was partially successful, as his army got stuck in the pestilent swamps of the Danube River. The second

---

[35] Ibid. p. 83.

expedition in 1043 was more successful, and Hungary was completely subjugated to the Holy Roman Empire.

Conflicts broke out, even within Germany itself, for the most insignificant reasons: a stolen cow, fields run over by hunters, sheltering a runaway serf, etc. All of these were perfect occasions for inciting violence within Germany. Low nobles would unite against their seniors, while senior nobles would do everything they could to ensure the subservience of their vassals.

Parish officials often came into conflict with neighboring feudal lords, who they believed took away their power and authority. This sort of atmosphere gave rise to the typical medieval landscape, consisting of small, highly fortified towns. Each monastery and each town had to fend for itself, often at the expense of its neighbors. Germany slipped into a sort of perennial war. Whole villages were burned down to punish their feudal lord while the lord sat within his fortifications. Neighbors became potential enemies, which impeded free trade and stifled the economy. It's likely that numerous famines stemmed from this state of anarchy, which made the transfer of information and goods between settlements nearly impossible.[36] At points, the famine was so drastic that it compelled people to resort to cannibalism. People were forced to eat bread made from infested grains, which resulted in epidemics of diseases, such as ergotism.[37] Other diseases also set foot in Europe, such as the black plague or leprosy

The cultural, social, and economic landscape of Henry's country was abysmal. Death was everywhere, and death came in the worst possible forms. It isn't surprising that people from all walks of life searched for a way out. They needed consolation, something that would convince them that their terrestrial suffering wasn't for nothing. Fortunately for them, the church was able to do this. By interpreting all these evils as punishments from above, the church gave people hope that they could improve things if they became good and pious people. Even though the Salians focused on the secular value of the church, the people recognized the spiritual value of the church. This revivified status of the

---

[36] Ibid.

[37] Ergot is a species of fungi that grows on grain, especially rye. The drug LSD is made from ergot. Up until recently, it wasn't uncommon for whole villages or even regions of a country to suffer from ergotism, which is characterized by gastrointestinal issues, gangrene, hallucinations, and psychosis.

church is another reason for the Investiture Crisis.

The church was perhaps the only institution to preach peace on Earth. While everything screamed war, the church murmured words of peace to the ears of the population. From this stemmed the church's Peace and Truce of God initiatives, not only in Germany but in all of Europe. People should not engage in warfare activities during certain periods of the year (such as important Christian holidays). In some regions, people abstained from warfare activities from Wednesday to Monday. Henry III, who understood the momentum of this collective movement, accepted it in 1043.

Perhaps the people of Europe didn't observe the Peace and Truce of God diligently enough, as the winter between 1045 and 1046 was exceedingly bitter, followed by famine and plague. Henry III fell ill, and it seemed as if Germany would have to seek a new emperor since Henry III only had a female child. However, Henry soon got better and continued with his ambitious plans for his empire. One of the things he did was ramp up simony and implicitly allow marriage among priests.[38] By doing this, he went against two important canons of the church. Marriage among priests wasn't unheard of, but this practice became even more frequent in the early 11th century. Positions in the church were bought and sold like any other commodity on the market. In Germany, elections within the church became insignificant and meaningless because someone could always make a good bid and take a certain post, often leaving it to his successors. Thus, simony and marriage among priests combined to make an absurd situation in which people would buy positions in the church hierarchy and then attempt to bequeath them to their children.

Coronation of Henry III and the Perpetuation of the Investiture Crisis

Henry III crossed the Alps in 1046, leading a sort of ecclesiastical army into Italy. He was welcomed by Pope Gregory VI, who had done a few things that angered Henry III, such as not appointing bishops liked by the imperial court. A council was held, which resulted in Gregory's dismissal. He was accused of simony, publicly shamed, and forced to step down from the papacy. The whimsical quality of Henry's ethical

---

[38]Simony is the practice of selling positions in the church hierarchy. Henry III was not the first nor the last German ruler to do this, but during his reign, simony reached new heights.

reasoning is obvious. In Germany, simony was rampant and somewhat encouraged by the court. In Italy, it was used to depose Pope Gregory VI.

A sort of mock papal elections were held. Ostensibly, the people of Rome were allowed to choose their new pope. However, they renounced this right and shifted it to none other than Henry III, who proclaimed the bishop of Bamberg, who was on very friendly terms with his court, as the new pope. He was named Pope Clement II. The new pope crowned Henry III and proclaimed him to be the Holy Roman emperor in 1046.[39]

In the next few days, it became clear that Henry III had amassed terrestrial and total spiritual power. He had the power to choose and depose important authorities within the hierarchy of the Roman Church. He could depose any pope he wanted and put his own German pope on the throne.

Returning to Germany, where a plethora of problems awaited him, he left Clement II in Rome, bringing the old pope, Gregory VI, with him. Gregory VI was put into a prison/castle situated on the banks of the Rhine. Clement II died in 1047, poisoned by the Romans (at least some speculated). The Holy Roman emperor chose a Bavarian named Poppo, Bishop of Brixen, to be the new pope. Poppo became Damasus II, but his stay in the chair of Saint Peter was exceedingly short; he died twenty-three days after being proclaimed as pope in 1048. He was likely poisoned by the anti-imperial party, whose members were still rather numerous in Rome.

Emperor Henry III then chose Bruno, Bishop of Toul, to be the next pope. Bruno took the name Leo IX. He knew that his personal power in Rome would be slight and that he had to come to some sort of agreement with the people and priests of Rome. He met and talked with the most important people of Rome before he even entered the city, and he took the position granted to him by the emperor. This placated the Romans, who accepted Leo IX.

Leo IX's papacy signified a sort of truce between Henry III and the church. However, the conflict wasn't fully solved, as the Investiture Crisis was simply moved to the side. Henry III returned to the main craft of the Salians: warfare. Conflicts with Hungarians, Slavs, Flemish, Italians,

---

[39]Zeller, Jules. L'empire germanique et l'Eglise au Moyen-Age: les Henri

and Poles kept Henry III busy. He fell ill and died in 1056, leaving the throne to his son, Henry IV.

Henry III was an extremely powerful ruler, possibly more powerful than Charlemagne and Otto the Great. He dominated numerous nations without really governing them. His power and influence depended on his personal energy and ability to quickly solve complex political issues, often thanks to his use of force. However, the problems he left to his successors were too heavy for them to bear. The Investiture Crisis, which became somewhat dormant during his reign, would reignite as soon as he died.

Henry IV was six years old when Henry III died, so he naturally needed a regent. His mother, Agnes, implored Pope Victor II to support her son and herself until Henry became mature enough to follow in his father's footsteps. In spite of receiving support from the church, Agnes couldn't maintain the same level of order within the empire. As soon as Henry III died, various nobles started to rebel. Agnes felt obliged to return numerous dukedoms to the high nobility, increasing their power and influence.

The increasing autonomy of the Italians shouldn't come as too much of a surprise. In 1058, Stephen IX was elected pope after the death of Victor II. The election happened without the knowledge of the imperial family. With a lot of reforms in mind (for instance, he foresaw the future choice of popes led by the cardinals, not by the emperor, the people, or the nobles of Rome), Stephen IX was deemed dangerous by numerous important players in Rome. He was assassinated soon after he rose to the papacy. In the chaos that ensued after the assassination, Benedict X became the new head of the Roman Church (he was actually an antipope, as his ascension wasn't legitimate). He rose to power thanks to intrigue and powerful connections; Benedict X was the brother of the much-hated but influential ex-Pope Benedict IX. The next pope, Nicholas II, was brought in by the supporters of the assassinated Stephen IX, who removed Antipope Benedict X in 1059. Benedict X could only cling to the papal throne for a short while; despite having powerful connections, the clergy simply wouldn't tolerate an antipope on the throne for a long time.[40]

---

[40]The antipope was essentially a pope who was later rejected by the Catholic Church as illegitimate. Benedict X was one such pope who was rejected by the Catholic Church.

Nicholas II was of immense importance for separating the church from the influence of the Holy Roman emperors. Pope Nicholas II confirmed the reforms initiated by Stephen IX, moving on to once and for all ban marriage among priests. He also incited people to reject priests known for their simony and licentious behavior. During the time of Nicholas II, it became clear that the pope could only be chosen by a council of cardinals and that the opinions of people, nobility, and the emperor himself could only come after the cardinals made their candidate known.

By this time, the numerous priests became so much like the commoners that they started carrying arms and amassing material possessions. Nicholas II reinstated the ban on weapons among priests and sought to limit private possession among church personnel. The communal spirit was enhanced by an obligation of group meals of all religious personnel serving within the same church. All these and many other obligations were proclaimed formally by the Council of Melfi in 1059.

Meanwhile, young Henry IV was growing up, with his responsibilities as the head of state being fulfilled by his mother. A group of influential aristocrats decided that young Henry should be guided and educated by serious church authorities, such as Bishop Anno. In 1062, Henry IV was kidnapped by Bishop Anno while he was staying with his mother in Kaiserswerth. As the story goes, the bishop visited Henry and Agnes in their palace at Kaiserswerth (modern-day Düsseldorf) and invited Henry for a boat ride on the Rhine. The boat ride turned out to be a kidnapping, and Henry IV came under the custody of Bishop Anno.

Anno was a different sort of pedagogue for the young Henry. While his mother ostensibly allowed for numerous indulgences, Anno was sterner and would often drive Henry to the brink of mental collapse with his disciplinary methods.[41] This sort of upbringing was too unstable and contributed to Henry IV becoming unstable. He was less than prepared to deal with the challenges of the Investiture Crisis and the internal strife in Germany.

In 1065, Henry IV reached the age of majority and started to rule the empire on his own. Henry IV wanted to revive the power of his father, which had been lost during the years of regency under his mother Agnes.

---

[41]Ibid. p. 236

He set about attempting to obtain the control of large fiefs and suppress the power of the high nobility, relying heavily on the low nobility, much like his father had. However, Henry IV had to face a much stronger church, which was led by a very important figure: Hildebrand.

You may recall that we talked about how Henry III exiled Pope Gregory VI, sending him to Germany. Hildebrand was one of the people who followed Gregory VI to Germany. Hildebrand slowly made his way up the ranks, thanks to his religious zeal, honesty, and tact. Hildebrand's efforts were recognized when he was appointed the archdeacon of the church around 1058. He led the administration of the church from then on and through the reigns of numerous popes.

By 1073, Hildebrand's popularity and influence were such that it almost allowed him to bypass the papal election laws that he himself set forth! As Pope Alexander II was being mourned by the people and clergy of Rome, the crowd started to shout Hildebrand's name, offering him up as the new pope. Hildebrand didn't want to be elected in this way. In fact, he fled the scene to avoid any irregularities. He was quickly found and elected by a council of cardinals and promptly hailed by the people of Rome. He became Pope Gregory VII, the name being chosen as an homage to his teacher, Pope Gregory VI. Gregory VII immediately set about reissuing bans of simony and marriage among priests, which were now serious offenses punishable by excommunication. Gregory VII also reaffirmed the exclusive papal right to elect bishops and move them across dioceses.

Needless to say, this wasn't really welcomed back in Germany. Henry IV wanted to do the exact opposite; he wanted the church to completely submit to him, and he wanted to control the elections of popes and bishops. But right about the time of Hildebrand's ascension to the chair of Saint Peter, the so-called Saxon rebellion broke out in Germany. Saxony had many powerful lords who felt threatened by the young and rash Henry IV, and they rebelled against their king around 1073. The conflict lasted for several years, seriously weakening Henry's power. By 1075, it had become clear that Henry's forces would prevail, and the young king could finally turn to the rebellious Italians. He then went blatantly against the laws promulgated by Gregory VII by appointing Tedald as the archbishop of Milan.

In 1076, the animosities between the Holy Roman Empire and the church reached new heights. Gregory VII was formally "deposed" by the

Synod of Worms, which consisted mainly of imperial-friendly German priests. In turn, Henry IV was excommunicated by Pope Gregory VII, which seriously endangered his status in the Holy Roman Empire. The rebellious counts and dukes (especially in Saxony) now had another argument against Henry IV. Seriously weakened and shaken by the excommunication, Henry was forced to seek penance from Gregory VII. In 1077, Henry IV journeyed to Canossa, where Gregory VII awaited him.[42] According to an old story, Henry kneeled for three days in front of Canossa Castle before being let in. By performing such a deed, Henry managed to wash away his previous sins, forcing Pope Gregory VII to forgive him for his previous wrongdoings.

Henry IV at Canossa.

Generally speaking, Gregory VII was ready to negotiate with Henry IV, even after Henry's subsequent and numerous breaches of agreements he made with the church. Henry did not openly or formally accept the new German king (or anti-king) Rudolf, who was chosen by the German nobility and supported by the church. By 1078, Gregory was regularly receiving angry letters from the Saxons, who renewed their

---

[42]Morrison, Karl F. "Canossa: a revision." Traditio 18 (1962): 121-148.

rebellion, spurred by Henry's recent problems with the church. They were perplexed by Gregory's ambiguous stance toward Henry and the new king, Rudolf, and didn't understand why Gregory continued to recognize Henry as the king of the Germans. The hesitancy continued well into 1080 when it became clear that Henry would prevail over Rudolf. Only then did Gregory express his support for Rudolf. He also renewed his excommunication of Henry, something that was not necessarily driven by military concerns. Henry continued to work with people who had already been excommunicated by the church. He tried to bribe a papal legate and continued behaving in a flagrant and impudent way.

Henry, in turn, deposed the pope via the Synod of Brexen, which was attended exclusively by bishops friendly to the Holy Roman Empire. The new pope was proclaimed as well. Archbishop Guibert became Antipope Clement III.

Henry managed to reach Rome by 1084, and Clement III was finally and formally proclaimed as the new pope. Gregory VII had no other choice but to flee the city. The same year, Clement III proclaimed Henry as the Holy Roman emperor. Both were soon forced to flee Rome due to the threat posed by the Norman forces that were friendly to Gregory VII. However, the old pope wasn't allowed to sit in the chair of Saint Peter, largely due to the disorder the Norman troops caused in Rome. Gregory VII was held responsible for this and was forced to flee once again.

Over the next twenty years or so, two lines of popes would be elected, one pro-imperial and the other anti-imperial. For the most part, the pro-imperials weren't really influential in Rome, but they sporadically made themselves known, even in Rome proper. The Investiture Crisis continued until the ascent of Henry V, the son of Henry IV, in 1105.

Henry IV returned to Germany, where he had a multitude of unsettled matters with aristocrats. These internal quarrels kept him busy in the last twenty years of his reign. The influence of Henry's son, Henry V, increased in the last few years of Henry IV's reign. Ultimately, Henry V obtained support from the nobility and forced his father to abdicate in 1105.

Henry V initially gave people the impression of a young man who wanted to resolve the conflict between the church and the empire. However, that opinion changed in 1111 when he imprisoned Pope

Paschal II, compelling the pope to give him the imperial crown. This started a conflict between the nobility and the church, which ended in the Concordat of Worms in 1121, which once and for all ended the Investiture Crisis.

The Concordat of Worms affirmed the pope's supremacy in the realm of the church, setting the scene for an unprecedented rise in the pope's power.[43] Henry V died at a fairly young age in 1125, and his death also ended the Salian dynasty.

[43]De Mesquita, Bruce Bueno. "Popes, Kings, and Endogenous Institutions: The Concordat of Worms and the Origins of Sovereignty." International Studies Review 2, no. 2 (2000): 93-118.

Chapter 5: The Hohenstaufen Emperors

With the dusk of Salian rule came the dawn of the Hohenstaufen dynasty. Progenitors of the Hohenstaufen dynasty had already come to prominence during the Ottonian dynasty. The Hohenstaufen family came from Swabia, and the heads of the family served as counts of the palace in Swabia. Frederick Hohenstaufen was one such count of the palace. In the 11th century, he managed to prepare the ground for his family's future rise to power. Count Frederick's son, Frederick of Büren, married a cousin of Pope Leo IX, which immensely improved the status of his family. Frederick of Büren had a son who ultimately became Frederick I, Duke of Swabia, in 1079 on the orders of Holy Roman Emperor Henry IV.

Frederick I, Duke of Swabia, married the daughter of Henry IV, Agnes, fostering the bonds between the rising Hohenstaufen family and the ruling Salian dynasty. Frederick I helped the Salians in their struggle within the province of Swabia. At the time, there were a number of powerful warlords (such as Rudolf of Rheinfelden, the anti-king) in Swabia who contested the authority of Salians. These warlords might have understood that the downfall of the Salians had already started, but they didn't get the timing right. Their revolt came too soon.

Frederick was succeeded, unsurprisingly, by another Frederick around 1105. Much like his father, Frederick II also closely followed the orders of the Salians.

With the death of Emperor Henry V in 1125, the Salian dynasty made its final appearance in the great historical drama. The power void had to be filled as soon as possible, and the choice ultimately fell to either Frederick II, Duke of Swabia, or Lothair of Supplinburg, Duke of Saxony. Frederick II must have pointed out that his mother, Agnes, was the daughter of Henry IV, which meant he had the imperial blood necessary for rising to the throne of the Holy Roman Empire. Lothair of Supplinburg, on the other hand, had the aristocracy on his side; all the imperial blood in the world didn't mean anything if one wasn't supported by the aristocracy.

Lothair was chosen by the members of the nobility in the elections that came immediately after Henry V's death in 1125. As was customary at the time, the new ruler had to assert his dominance within Germany itself. Lothair had the Hohenstaufens against him. Frederick II lost to Lothair in the royal elections and also faced the prospect of losing some of his lands due to Lothair's policies. It was only natural for armed conflict to break out due to such issues.

Another civil war ensued, in which Lothair's side prevailed, making Lothair of Supplinburg not only the new German king but also the new Holy Roman emperor in 1133. Lothair's tenure was a sort of interregnum, a short span that came in between two dynasties (in this case, the Salians and Hohenstaufens).

Although Lothair didn't really rule for a long time, he was instrumental in one of the schisms that happened within the Catholic Church. In 1130, Innocent II and Anacletus II both claimed to be legitimately chosen heads of the church, and neither would back down. Innocent II was driven away from Rome by supporters of Anacletus II, but he managed to obtain the support of major European rulers, including Lothair.

Perhaps one of the clauses of Lothair's support for Innocent II was the latter crowning him as the Holy Roman emperor in 1131. Some five years later, Lothair succeeded in finding an agreement with the German aristocrats, but he died shortly after, in 1137, leaving the succession question open since he had no direct male successors.

Conrad III Hohenstaufen

At this historical moment, Conrad III Hohenstaufen stepped onto the scene after being elected as the new German king in 1138. In the first few years of his reign, Conrad III had to face rivals, such as Lothair's cousins, Henry the Proud and Henry the Lion, with the matter being settled by 1142.

Conrad III was a typical German ruler. He was rugged, warlike, ambitious, and energetic. He was taken aback when he heard priests preaching in favor of the Second Crusade. After extensive preparations, he set the course for the Holy Land in 1147, bringing a large army with him. The future Holy Roman emperor, Frederick Barbarossa, followed his uncle Conrad III on this crusade.

King Conrad III.

The Germans were led through Hungary, the Balkans, and the Byzantine Empire before finally reaching the Holy Land.[44] Although the Germans encountered mainly Christians, there are many testimonies of their less-than-laudable behavior. For instance, it is said that German troops regularly stole food and other products from the local populations and engaged in numerous small skirmishes and street fights with angry sellers. Word about the Crusaders' barbaric behavior soon spread throughout the Byzantine Empire, with market deals between local populations and Crusaders being completed over thick town walls. Philippopolis, a city in Thrace (modern-day Bulgaria and, at the time, a settlement within the Byzantine Empire), saw similar scenes. The German army was stationed outside of the city, and some soldiers found their way to a tavern, where they proceeded to drink large quantities of alcohol and get into a scuffle with a snake charmer, who they believed tried to poison them.[45]

In Adrianople, the situation was similar. Prior to the arrival of the main group of German armies, a German noble stopped to rest and recuperate in a monastery close to Adrianople, only to be murdered by robbers or soldiers who happened to be there. When the main group of German forces arrived, King Conrad ordered his nephew Frederick to sack the monastery and find the culprits. The excessive force with which Frederick's troops inflicted revenge called for the intervention of the Byzantine Empire, though the Germans soon continued their march toward the Holy Land.

The Germans faced other events as well. At one point, while camping in the plain called Choirobacchoi, the whole army was surprised by a flash flood. Numerous soldiers died in this incident, and many more lost their equipment and provisions. The Byzantines considered this to be a divine intervention, similar to that of the drowning of the Egyptian army in the Red Sea.

However, the Germans continued marching, soon reaching Constantinople. The people in the city, including Byzantine Emperor Manuel, were wary about the intentions of the Germans and made the necessary preparations for a potential attack. The city's garrison was fostered, and the famous walls of Constantinople were strengthened.

---

[44] Roche, Jason T. "King Conrad III in the Byzantine Empire: A Foil for Native Imperial Virtue." (2015).
[45] Roche, Jason T. "King Conrad III in the Byzantine Empire: A Foil for Native Imperial Virtue."

Battle of Inab, Second Crusade.

The Germans didn't attempt to conquer Constantinople, and they were able to cross the Bosphorus in relative peace and order. However, the Second Crusade was a general failure, with the Germans and French being defeated by the Seljuk Turks and failing to capture Damascus. The Second Crusade ended in 1149, with the major protagonists returning home. Fairly soon after returning, in 1152, Frederick was crowned king of the Germans in Aachen, shortly after the death of King Conrad III. King Conrad had recognized Frederick's potential and also acknowledged that his own son, Conrad, was still too young to become king. Conrad sought to avoid some of the mistakes of past kings and emperors. He didn't leave any space for the regent period, where the royal power was usually diluted.

The young King Frederick was immediately put in a position to assert his royal authority and administer justice impartially. As the story goes, a knight, accused of some criminal acts that seriously endangered his reputation, came to Frederick during the celebration of his coronation and started imploring the new king to pardon him for his misdeeds. The young king remained unmoved by the knight's plight and decided that justice should not be bent to suit individual whims.[46] This is a perfect example of medieval royal justice, which was quite often delivered personally and publicly by the king himself.

Barbarossa excelled in these matters, often participating in disputes between dukes, counts, and princes and settling feuds that had been going on for a long time. This proved instrumental in establishing his reputation and granted him the title of *pater patriae* ("father of the fatherland"). Barbarossa wasn't simply a powerful German leader. He was also a fairly wise man, someone who would gladly try to settle disputes between local lords to foster the growth of the kingdom.

Frederick Barbarossa

One of Frederick's initial moves was to sign the Treaty of Constance in 1153, which was, in a way, his show of respect for the pope. As was the case with many other German leaders, Frederick Barbarossa vowed to defend the pope's interest in Italy in case anyone tried to go against it, such as the Byzantine Empire, which still wanted a piece of southern Italy.

Frederick also went through the usual ordeal of having to reconquer Italy. On the wings of the Treaty of Constance and a renewed respect for the pope, Frederick marched into Italy with his army in 1154, sacking and looting a few cities, such as Tortona. The aim of this Italian expedition was to finally bring Sicily within the pope's sphere of influence.

As you may remember, Sicily had been under the command of the Saracens (Muslim Arabs) who dared to cross into mainland Italy. By the time of Frederick Barbarossa, the Muslims had been pushed out of Sicily, only to be replaced with insubordinate Normans, who were avid adventurers and incredibly good soldiers. The aim of Frederick's first Italian expedition was to push the Normans out. In this respect, Frederick's first Italian expedition was a failure because he was forced to return to Germany in 1155 due to unrest that started to unravel there.

---

[46]Weiler, B. (2009). The King as Judge: Henry II and Frederick Barbarossa as Seen by Their Contemporaries. In Challenging the Boundaries of Medieval History: The Legacy of Timothy Reuter (pp. 115-140).

Barbarossa (middle) with his two children.

Frederick's first Italian expedition also resulted in him being crowned as the Holy Roman emperor, something that was, of course, part of the inevitable tit for tat between him and the pope. As mentioned, Frederick's job in Italy was far from complete, so he was forced to cut his military expedition short and return to Italy. The Normans were still a threat, which was why Pope Adrian IV sought negotiations with the Normans. This left Barbarossa very displeased and strained his relationship with the pope. Moreover, word reached Frederick Barbarossa that somewhere in Rome hung a picture of Emperor Lothair receiving the imperial crown from the pope. It was obvious in this picture that the pope had the upper hand and that Lothair was merely receiving the pope's divine wisdom and power. This picture remained in place despite Frederick's orders to remove it.

The stage was thus set for another Italian campaign. By 1158, Frederick was once again in Italy with his army. This didn't go well with the cities in northern Italy, which were used to being plundered with each German campaign in Italy. The revolt, this time, came to a tipping point in Milan, which sought to assert itself in the region of Lombardy. Milan and other cities in Lombardy took matters into their own hands, executing power that Frederick believed was rightfully reserved only for him.[47]

Frederick felt obliged to punish Milan for such behavior and started by besieging a close ally of Milan, Crema. The siege of Crema lasted from 1159 to 1160 and ended with excessive violence and the sacking of the city. During the long siege of Crema, a lot of prisoners were killed on both sides in an endless stream of retributions. Frederick even tied some hostages to his siege equipment so they wouldn't be targeted by the defenders from Crema. Whether this tactic worked or not, Frederick ultimately burst into Crema, destroying it completely while sparing the citizens.

A similar fate awaited Milan. First, Frederick sent a special envoy to Milan. He took one of the Milanese hostages he had at his disposal and pulled out one of his eyes. The hostage was then sent to Milan just so that the people knew what was waiting for them around the corner.[48] The subsequent siege of Milan in 1161 was particularly bitter. During the winter of 1161/62, Frederick cut all roads leading to Milan and barred anyone from entering or exiting the city. Eventually, the starved population gave in and surrendered. The citizens were brought out, and the city was razed.

It goes without saying that Frederick Barbarossa experienced the same sort of troubles in Italy as his predecessors had. In the 12th century, a number of Italian cities experienced major social shifts, moving away from the feudal system. Italian cities, which were culturally and

---

[47]Velov, Ivana. Literary And Historical Interpretation Of Frederick Barbarossa's Conquest Of The Italian Communes: Analysis Of The Events And Personalities Described In The Novel" Baudolino" By Umberto Eco. *Дипломатија И Безбедност*, 249.
[48]Ibid.

technologically advanced, provided opportunities relatively unavailable to the average German serf. Commerce and quality craftsmanship made for bustling city markets, and some people started amassing serious capital. Artisans made high-quality products, with prices dictated by associations of artisans, which grew increasingly influential, not only in Italian cities but also throughout Europe.

Such cities demanded freedom and would never fully accept any of the German kings who entered Italy. Perhaps they might have accepted him if he had been Italian. But during this period, the Germans had the military advantage, so the Italians were doomed to being constantly conquered by what they perceived to be barbaric Germans. And they were right in recognizing that the Germans were bringing an entirely different culture and system with them.

The conflicts with Italy would continue for quite some time. In 1176, the hostilities temporarily stopped. The Italians managed to inflict a decisive defeat and repel Frederick Barbarossa in the Battle of Legnano.[49] By this time, Frederick was facing a highly organized revolt, which had materialized in the form of the Lombard League, heralded by the rebuilt Milan. This time, Frederick's forces were fairly weak and scattered throughout Italy. The previous Italian expeditions didn't go well, and the nobles were increasingly reluctant to participate in another pointless Italian expedition. Epidemics would often break out in the army during these expeditions, decimating the already weakened morale of the troops. This was the major reason why Frederick arrived with a somewhat smaller body of men in comparison to his earlier exploits.

His forces throughout Italy attempted to achieve subordination to his rule. In 1176, Barbarossa was waiting for his reinforcements, led by Philip of Cologne, to arrive. Barbarossa was stationed in Pavia (near Milan) and was moving north to Como to meet the arriving reinforcements. This was a risky move since all these maneuvers were well within the range of the forces stationed in Milan and its environs. It is likely that, together with his reinforcements, Barbarossa had around three thousand men. His forces were made up almost exclusively of cavalry units.

---

[49]FRANKE, Daniel. From Defeat to Victory in Northern Italy: Comparing Staufen Strategy and Operations at Legnano and Cortenuova, 1176-1237. *Nuova Antologia Militare*, 2021, 2.5: 27.

Barbarossa left Pavia with around one thousand cavalrymen, leaving a small regiment in Pavia itself. He headed north to meet Philip of Cologne in Como. The Italians might have numbered up to fifteen thousand men, mostly infantry. After merging with the reinforcements, Barbarossa headed back to Pavia. His path was blocked by a large force of the Lombard League. Imperial forces were drawn by Lombardian cavalry into battle, with the main body of Barbarossa's forces being gradually surrounded by the much larger Lombardian army. Carnage ensued, and Barbarossa just barely made it back to Pavia. It's said that Empress Beatrice had already started mourning him when Barbarossa arrived in Pavia.

The defeat at Legnano practically drove Barbarossa out of Italy, though he did have some pockets of support. He was forced to accept the Peace of Venice in 1177, as well as the Peace of Constance in 1183, both of which were favorable to the Lombard League. The Germans had lost the upper hand in Italy, but they were free to focus on other conquests. The Third Crusade, Frederick's second, would turn out to be his last military endeavor.

Barbarossa's Policies

Unlike some of his predecessors, namely the Ottonians and Salians, Frederick Barbarossa was on much better terms with the nobility, or at least he knew how to manage the nobles so that they didn't question his power in a violent way.[50] He was, as mentioned, a fair judge in resolving disputes, for instance, between Henry the Lion and Henry Jasomirgott, very early on in his career. Another important early move was the destruction of the castles of nobles who dared to try and make the most out of Barbarossa's absence in 1154 and 1155.

The economy also saw some improvements during Frederick Barbarossa's reign. Prior to his rule, there were only around twenty-five mints across Germany. Barbarossa left a total of 215 mints in Germany after his death.[51] He was a skilled businessman and a great negotiator. At one point, the people of Cologne came into a dispute with the archbishop of Cologne. The people of Cologne wanted to make some changes to the public spaces, but they found a powerful opponent in the

---

[50]Friederich A. Warlord or Financial Strategist: Frederick Barbarossa. Johns Hopkins University. 2022 Nov 10;3(1).
[51]Ibid.

form of Philip von Heinsberg. The emperor had to step in and settle the dispute. Barbarossa decided that the people were right in wanting to change their public space, but they had to pay a certain sum to their local church. In turn, the church couldn't just spend this money; it was obliged to invest it in some lucrative business endeavors with high rates of return.

Barbarossa was no stranger to debt and would sometimes even pawn off royal property so that he could obtain money as fast as possible. However, he was also very good at obtaining money. For instance, he insisted on taxing imperial churches and claimed the properties of dead clergymen. This gave rise to some funny scenes; instead of letting their money go automatically to Barbarossa after their death, some clergymen preferred to give it away. Customs and tolls were another important source of income for Barbarossa's administration.

Occasionally, other less laudable ways of obtaining money were employed. The Jews in Germany were accused of numerous crimes for which they were fined. Funnily enough, Barbarossa fined another gentleman, Philip, Archbishop of Cologne, for extorting the Jews. Barbarossa recognized the power of fines. There were hefty fines for not showing up at the councils he organized, and the fines were especially high for the nobility.

Barbarossa would also sometimes sell his exclusive right to govern certain areas, the so-called regalia. Regalia included things like the right to levy different kinds of taxes, such as market tolls, wagon tolls, forage taxes, gate tolls, and transit tolls. Regalia also included the right to control mills, bridges, and fisheries. Finally, those who were ready to pay good money to Barbarossa for their regalia could levy the standard annual tax on property, as well as an interesting and a bit frightening "tax on persons."[52]

Depending on the political situation and the need for money, Barbarossa would sometimes accept large payments instead of besieging and occupying a city. This was especially prevalent in Italy's wealthy north, where Genoa and Pisa paid good money to Barbarossa, who, in turn, had to grant them ownership of Sardinia.

Barbarossa's numerous conquests and military victories can only be understood by looking at his careful money management and strong

[52]Ibid.

business sense.

Third Crusade, Barbarossa Death, and the Decline of the Hohenstaufen Dynasty

The Muslims managed to take over Jerusalem in 1187, sending shockwaves through the whole of Europe. The Second Crusade, as we've seen, has left a number of questions unanswered. The Arabs weren't in any way defeated, and the Christian regions in the Middle East were doomed to be slowly ground down by the Arabs. One of the major successes of the Crusaders, namely the capture of Jerusalem, was negated by Sultan Saladin and his forces. Three European leaders— Richard I the Lionheart, Philip II of France, and Frederick Barbarossa— agreed to embark on the Third Crusade. Richard the Lionheart and Philip II preferred the naval route, while Barbarossa took the land route, which ultimately cost him his life.

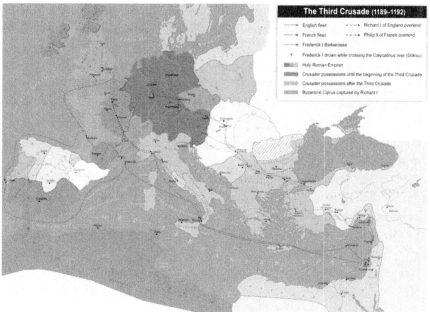

Holy Roman Empire in the late reign of Barbarossa, as well as Barbarossa's path toward the Holy Land.

It is interesting that already in the 12th century, there was a sort of separation between England, France, and the Holy Roman Empire with respect to their naval actions. Namely, England and France were starting to use the sea to their advantage more and more, while the Germans preferred to stay on land. This separation remained in the centuries to come, and the Germans never really became a "naval nation" like the French and especially the English.

Barbarossa first had to ensure the safe passage of his army through Hungary and the Byzantine Empire. King Bela III of Hungary granted safe passage, as did Byzantine Emperor Isaac II Angelos. Money was always a source of worry for Barbarossa, and this was certainly true in the case of the Third Crusade. His soldiers were forced to help themselves along the way, and Barbarossa even managed to strike a deal with Isaac II, who allowed Barbarossa's forces to gather fruit and vegetables they came across in the Byzantine Empire. This deal wasn't really welcomed by the populations who directly encountered the Germans, though, so numerous skirmishes and scuffles broke out along the way.

Sometimes, the locals tried to profit from the Crusaders by offering criminally bad exchange rates. Currency exchange back in the day was still a novel thing, and it was very challenging to come up with a fixed, fair rate. The exchange rate was thus left to chance and the whims of the locals, who sometimes took advantage of the fact the Crusaders often had no other choice but to buy their products. This further complicated the already tense relationship between the Germans and the Byzantines.

Also, the Byzantines didn't look favorably upon the military presence of Germans in the Balkans. The Serbs and Bulgarians already had their own states in the Balkans and were trying to expand their sphere of influence. Barbarossa was in contact with the Serbian zupan (supreme leader or grand prince) Stefan Nemanja. Barbarossa's army was warmly welcomed by Stefan Nemanja. The Germans received food, such as grain, livestock, and wine. The nobles were lavished with luxurious gifts.[53]

After passing through Bulgaria and a long stay in Philippopolis, the Germans reached the region of Constantinople. After a lot of back and forth and a lot of drama, the Byzantine emperor agreed to ferry the Germans from Europe to Asia Minor (modern-day western Turkey). As

---

[53]Frederick I. The Crusade of Frederick Barbarossa: The History of the Expedition of the Emperor Frederick and Related Texts. Ashgate Publishing, Ltd.; 2010.
This manuscript is a collection of works written immediately after the Third Crusade and later copies of these early works. Its authorship is a fairly complicated issue, especially due to the fact that only portions of the early texts remain; for the rest, we have to rely on much later copies of early works.

they traveled eastward, the Germans encountered numerous unpleasant scenes. Besides the cultural differences, there were also religious differences, all of which gave rise to animosities between the Germans and their unwelcoming hosts.[54]

Once in the area held by the Muslims, the Germans encountered the Seljuk Turks, one of the many ethnic groups roaming the regions of the Middle East and allies of the Arabs, who were gaining the upper hand in the Middle East. The Turks occasionally harassed the German army, setting up ambushes and skirmishes, even though the Germans expected a peaceful reception since the Turks previously agreed to let the Germans pass through their lands.

The Germans were exhausted, having passed through a fairly arid region with little food. On April 30th, 1190, the Germans left their camp, and Turks quickly captured it in the hopes of gaining good loot. However, the Germans turned back and crushed the unsuspecting Turks. Two days later, there was another battle between the Germans and Turks. This time, the dukes of Swabia and Merania, as well as the counts of Kyburg and Oettingen, distinguished themselves by showcasing admirable valor on the battlefield. Count Kyburg is said to have killed seventeen men, a deed worthy of Homer's Achilles.

The Bohemians also proved to be worthy soldiers of Christ. Low on provisions, the Bohemians had to go out of the camp and forage. The Turks were diligently waiting for small groups of Germans to exit the camp in search of food. So, six Bohemian nobles put their armor on and then some servants' clothes. From afar, they might have looked like fairly large servants. In any case, they fooled the Turks, who rushed to attack them. The Bohemians quickly drew their concealed weapons and slashed the six opportunistic Turks.[55]

On May 3rd, the Germans were faced with a difficult situation. A Turkish prisoner was coerced into helping the Germans choose the best option. Either they would continue their passage through the desert or take a detour through a mountainous but more favorable region. The Germans started their climb in the mountains of Pisidia (the Taurus

---

[54]The cultural difference between Greeks and Germans moves along the same lines as the difference between Italians and Germans.
[55]Frederick I. The Crusade of Frederick Barbarossa: The History of the Expedition of the Emperor Frederick and Related Texts. Ashgate Publishing, Ltd.; 2010. P. 102

Mountains). The Turks knew the terrain better and would strategically place themselves above the Germans and shower them with stones and arrows. The heavy German armor came in handy here, though many were injured. Even the duke of Swabia was injured by a stone, and a knight named Werner was killed.[56] The Germans nevertheless managed to climb up to the Turks and eliminate them.

Just how perilous and dangerous the Crusades were is nicely showcased by the difficulties the Germans encountered along their way. They hadn't even arrived in the Holy Land yet; in fact, they had a long way to go, but they already participated in numerous small battles, their forces slowly being ground down. A few days after the events in the Pisidia mountains, on May 6th, 1190, another distinguished knight, Frederick of Hausen, died, not in battle but after falling off a horse.

Early depiction of Barbarossa during the Third Crusade.
https://commons.wikimedia.org/w/index.php?curid=6433070

About a month following this event, on June 10th, another tragedy struck the German army. Barbarossa was marching with his army through the region of Seleucia (modern-day southern Turkey). A major part of the army took a mountain pass to find a safe passage across the Saleph River. Barbarossa, tired of the endless Turkish mountains and drained by the heat, decided to swim across the Saleph in spite of warnings from his entourage that the river had a very strong flow. It should also be mentioned that Barbarossa was around sixty-seven years old at the time. He entered the river and soon drowned, although

---

[56]Ibid. p. 102

scholars don't know how exactly that happened.

The duke of Swabia, Barbarossa's own son, immediately became the head of the German army. Although seriously shaken by the death of their emperor, the Germans marched on toward the Holy Land. Ultimately, this crusade saw some successes, with Saladin's forces being pushed on several fronts. However, Jerusalem remained in Saladin's hands. The European armies finally returned home in 1192.

Barbarossa was succeeded by his second oldest son, Henry VI, who formally was the king of Germany for some time before his father's death. Henry was careful to first negotiate peace with the Italians, who were happy enough to crown him the Holy Roman emperor in 1191. Henry was known to be a highly educated man, much more so than his father, but he wasn't less cruel or warlike. He continued to hamper relationships with the Byzantine Empire and managed to extort a lot of money from the Byzantine emperor, threatening to invade it unless Germany received a hefty payment.

Henry VI died in 1197 at a fairly young age while preparing for the next crusade. In spite of trying hard to do so, Henry VI never managed to legitimize the hereditary monarchy. So, after his death, there was another interregnum period, which ultimately ended the short rule of the Hohenstaufen dynasty.

Chapter 6: The Great Interregnum Period

The unsolvable conundrum of succession has led to periods of disorganization and struggles for supremacy in many cases throughout history. The same scenario, combined with the prevarications of the Roman clergy, resulted in a period of instability and conflict in the Holy Roman Empire in the 13th century. The beginning of the Hohenstaufen dynasty's decline started to become evident with Emperor Henry VI's death in 1197. Before his passing, Henry designated his son Frederick as the heir to the Kingdom of Sicily and bequeathed the imperial throne to him as well. Frederick II was only three years old at the time of his father's death, and the fact that such a young heir was about to ascend to the throne emboldened aristocrats who were hostile to the Hohenstaufen dynasty.

One of the most influential popes of the Middle Ages, Innocent III, was drawn into these political events as soon as he ascended the papal throne in 1198. The late Emperor Henry came into possession of vast territories in Sicily that the pope considered to be his own. Pope Innocent took young Frederick under his protection and supported his claim to the Kingdom of Sicily, hoping that the youngster would hand these territories back to the church.

Amid the uproar in Germany that followed the death of Emperor Henry, Henry's brother, Philip of Swabia, issued a charter declaring that he would act on behalf of the newly appointed King Frederick to quell the impending conflict.[57] In the meantime, reluctant nobles took the opportunity to elect Otto IV, known by historians as an anti-king. Otto was the son of a former Saxon and Bavarian duke, and he was the nephew of Richard the Lionheart. Therefore, he enjoyed the support of John, the reigning king of England. Philip, on the other hand, had the support of Philip II of France, which further aggravated the impending conflict between France and England. A division in the Holy Roman Empire, created by the emergence of the two candidates, triggered a civil war that would last a decade.

Pope Innocent exerted a wide influence, claiming supremacy over all of Europe's kings. He successfully organized the Fourth Crusade in 1202, which resulted in the sack of Constantinople. He played an important role in the dispute between the two kings. He was originally sympathetic to Otto IV, but the German anti-king was not as enthusiastic about an alliance with the pope. Half-heartedly, Innocent III sought an alliance with Otto's rival, Philip. It seemed that this alliance would put an end to the conflict, but Philip's assassination in 1208 in Bamberg turned out to end the war.[58] The circumstances of Philip's death led to controversies and various theories. It is believed by some that Otto of Wittelsbach, who assassinated him, acted on behalf of the supporters of Otto IV. It is important to note that there is no agreement among experts regarding these assertions.

After Philip's death, Otto was determined to destroy Italy in case he didn't receive the imperial crown. As he remained the only candidate, Pope Innocent III had no choice but to crown him a year later. As all this was happening, Frederick II came to maturity and started to spread his influence in Sicily. Since the pope could not rely on an alliance with Otto, against whom he had only recently fought, young Frederick was the only viable option for him to try and achieve his interests.[59] Otto himself felt safer on the throne and did not feel the need to yield to the pope's entreaties. At the Battle of Bouvines in 1214, Otto faced a major defeat against a coalition of forces from France, Flanders, and parts of the Holy Roman Empire. Otto's influence and position were weakened after this battle, and he was eventually deposed in 1215. He withdrew to his hereditary lands of Brunswick, where he died in 1218. The throne was

[57]Bryce, James, *The Holy Roman Empire*, MacMillan and Company, 1866. 232
[58]Painter, Sidney, *A History of the Middle Ages 284-1500*, The MacMillan Press LTD, 1973. 326
[59]Holmes, George, *The Oxford History of Medieval Europe*, Oxford University Press, 1988. 225

left for Frederick to claim, and he was eventually crowned emperor.[60] Pope Innocent's plan to reunite Sicily with the rest of the Papal States didn't go as he had hoped, though. By supporting a Hohenstaufen claimant, he achieved the opposite: Sicily was united with the rest of the Holy Roman Empire, further cementing Hohenstaufen authority in the city and surrounding lands.

Frederick remained in Germany for about five years but only in order to organize the kingdom so that he only had to intervene in internal affairs as little as possible. On two occasions, in 1220 and 1232, he granted bishops and nobles some customary rights and gave them legal sovereignty in their own territories. He gave princes, dukes, and counts almost everything they asked for. He even went as far as to imprison his own son for trying to establish stricter governance by resisting the demands of the nobles.[61]

Frederick could have become one of the more capable rulers of his time, which he proved by consolidating his power and influence in Sicily. However, he did not seem to have the enthusiasm to extend this to the rest of the empire, thus laying the foundation for the rise of local rulers. He spent the rest of his reign traveling and did not concern himself much with the empire's internal affairs. His jurisdiction was limited to cities that were directly dependent on the imperial crown.

Hohenstaufen coat of arms.

[60]Painter, Sidney, *A History of the Middle Ages 284-1500,* The MacMillan Press LTD, 1973. 326
[61]Ibid. 327

Frederick promised the pope his participation in the Fifth Crusade (1217–1221) and vowed to aid Andrew II of Hungary and Leopold VI of Austria in their quest. In return for this promise, he expected to be granted imperial rights over certain cities in Italy. These imperialistic attempts led to the renewal of the Lombard League.[62]

Member cities of the Lombard Leagues

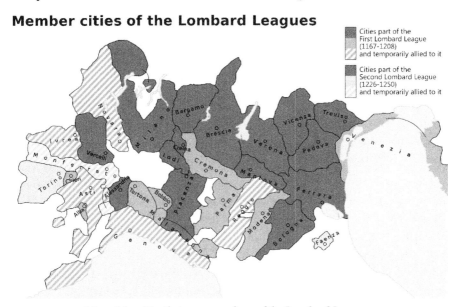

Map of the cities that were members of the Lombard League.
By Medhelan, CC BY-SA 4.0 <https://creativecommons.org/licenses/by-sa/4.0>, via Wikimedia Commons,
https://commons.wikimedia.org/wiki/File:Member_Cities_of_the_Lombard_Leagues.png

Frederick withdrew his claims, realizing the power of the Lombard League. Because of his mixed heritage (he had Norman and Flemish roots) and his frequent travels, Frederick considered himself a cosmopolite. His ties to the Muslim community, whom he welcomed in Rome, weren't welcomed by the clergy. Frederick tried to impose his worldview in Sicily and other parts of Italy and the Holy Roman Empire. These tendencies were in direct contrast with the church, which led to a rather unpleasant relationship between the emperor and the popes, most notably Pope Gregory IX. Although Frederick eventually fulfilled his promise and launched what he considered to be a successful crusade

---

[62] The Lombard League was an alliance between the acting pope and certain noblemen against the emperor, which proved to be efficient in the conflict against Frederick's grandfather Barbarossa a few decades prior.

(1228–1229), Pope Gregory IX wasn't satisfied with Frederick's ideas and his disinterest in the matters of the church. Frederick set a precedent, having achieved a successful crusade without the pope's involvement.[63] Pope Gregory IX excommunicated the unfavorable emperor, and this rivalry extended to both of their successors.

After a long and eventful reign, Frederick's death in 1250 marked the end of the rule of the Hohenstaufen dynasty. After his death, Frederick's supporters recognized the late sovereign's son, Conrad IV, as the rightful heir to the German throne, but other electors did not give their acquiescence. Due to Frederick's excommunication, which extended to his successor, the power in the Holy Roman Empire transitioned to rival kings of Germany who supported the pope. The first to be backed up by Pope Innocent IV was Henry Raspe, who died a few months after his election, leaving William, Count of Holland, to succeed him.

Despite Conrad's attempts to reconcile with the pope, no agreement was reached, and Conrad was excommunicated. He sought to assert control over the Kingdom of Sicily, ultimately planning to develop his influence from there as his father did before him. Conrad's four-year-long reign came to an end with his death during a military campaign in Italy. Frederick II's illegitimate son, Manfred, and Conrad's son, Conradin, replaced the late king and continued the struggle with the papacy, although they were unsuccessful. Manfred and Pope Urban IV negotiated for over two years. The pope offered Manfred recognition of his kingdom in exchange for his support in regaining Constantinople.

In 1263, Pope Urban IV issued an official regulation stating that the right to elect a king, although an age-old custom among the Germans, now officially belonged to the seven electors. The three archbishops of Mentz, Trier, and Cologne, the pastors of the oldest and richest dioceses in Germany, represented the German Church and had, for centuries, played a leading role in the elections. The other four electors were the dukes of Franconia, Swabia, Saxony, and Bavaria.[64]

---

[63]The results of the Sixth Crusade are not universally acclaimed, although Frederick proclaimed its success to Henry III of England.

[64]Bryce, James, *The Holy Roman Empire,* MacMillan and Company, 1866. 241

Seven prince-electors, Balduineum picture chronicle.

Pope Urban IV's successor, Pope Clement IV, provided continuity in the negotiations with Manfred when he became king of Sicily, where most of the Hohenstaufen influence still remained. Dissatisfied with Manfred's leadership in Sicily, Pope Clement IV sought help outside of Germany and Italy. First, he tried to gain support from King Henry III of England. The pope offered the Sicilian throne to Henry's son, Edmund of Lancaster, but some English nobles openly opposed this offer. King Henry's planned expedition to Sicily was thwarted by rebellious barons and required Pope Clement to seek alternatives. He sought help from King Louis IX of France, specifically from his brother, Charles I, Count of Anjou and Provence. Charles proved to be a competent leader; he defeated Manfred's army in the Battle of Benevento in 1266. Manfred himself refused to flee and died on the battlefield. Charles took control of Sicily, where he was crowned king by the pope.[65]

The imperial rule had largely declined by this time. The Holy Roman Empire looked more like an interwoven network of small territories

[65]Painter, Sidney, *A History of the Middle Ages 284-1500*, The MacMillan Press LTD, 1973. 329

ruled by kings, princes, dukes, counts, and other nobles. They all attempted to dominate certain areas, increase their sphere of influence, and make life harder for their rivals.

As the Norman Kingdom of Sicily became independent again and was subject to the House of Anjou, the pope fostered his control within the Papal States. Aside from the Papal States, the rest of Italy was without a centralized leadership, and there was constant conflict between local nobles and leaders. Burgundy and the surrounding provinces came under the overwhelming influence of France.

The greatest unrest in the Holy Roman Empire was mainly concentrated in Germany. The first to be elected as anti-king in Germany after the fall of the Hohenstaufens was William of Holland, who was crowned at Aachen, although he faced opposition from the Swabian party. The count palatine of the Rhine was excluded from taking part in the election on the grounds that he was under sentence of excommunication as a supporter of Conrad IV. A few of the remaining Hohenstaufen supporters claimed that William lacked courage and chivalrous qualities. Despite this, William managed to enjoy an unchallenged reign from 1254 to 1256.[66]

The electors eventually deemed him unfit, and a new foreign candidate emerged. In a sort of double election, the son of English King John, Richard of Cornwall, became the king of the Romans in 1257, receiving four out of seven votes from the electors. Richard was viewed as a compromise candidate, as he was seen as being capable enough to reconcile internal divisions within the empire. Soon, the electors found out that Richard had offered an unequal bribe to some of them before the election. So, their allegiance shifted to Alfonso X of Castile, who claimed succession to the Hohenstaufen dynasty through his mother, one of the daughters of Philip of Swabia.[67]

Richard had to return to England due to deteriorating relations between his brother, King Henry II, and the English barons. King Henry attempted to reform the legal and judicial systems and demanded increased taxes, which was the primary source of discontent among the barons. During his absence, Richard's supporters succeeded in expelling

[66]Wilson, Peter H. *Heart of Europe: A History of the Holy Roman Empire*. Harvard University Press, 2016. 548
[67]Bryce, James, *The Holy Roman Empire*, MacMillan and Company, 1866, 214

Conradin, the grandson of Frederick II and the last true Hohenstaufen, from Italy. Conradin was captured by Charles, who was king of Italy, at the Battle of Tagliacozzo in 1268. The battle that took place was the final display of power by the Hohenstaufen family. Conradin was held captive for three months in Naples until Charles decreed his fate: beheading.

While there are reports claiming that the pope disapproved of the atrocious treatment of Conradin committed during Conradin's imprisonment, there are also statements suggesting that Pope Clement IV might have given his approval or even suggested Conradin's execution in 1268.[68] Judges wouldn't concur with the sentence, but being backed by the pope, Charles went through with the public beheading in the marketplace of the town square of Naples. After Conradin's death, the situation in Germany changed in such a way that it became more favorable for Richard to return. He ruled for a short time before being forced to return to England, where he died in 1272.

Conradin's death as the last Hohenstaufen claimant secured the pope's main goal of maintaining his domain over Sicily and Naples, keeping them separate from the Holy Roman Empire.[69] In short, the popes, aided by the electors, triumphed over the Holy Roman emperors, and the empire lost its power.[70]

The conditions in Germany during that time were extremely poor and unpleasant. The German nobility was constantly appointing two opposing representatives with no real power for either side. The conflicts and power struggles between these candidates and their supporters contributed to the instability of the period. This was the height of the disarray and chaos in Germany during the Great Interregnum (named this way to distinguish it from the shorter period between 924 and 962). Disgruntled and power-thirsty dukes and barons attempted to expand their dominions through wars. Robbers swarmed the rivers and roads, and violence was the order of the day everywhere in the empire. There was a tendency for German society to return to this "natural condition of mankind" characterized by chronic war, to use the much later expression of Thomas Hobbes. Trade and commerce were disrupted, and the lack of a stable political environment made it challenging to establish

[68]Bryce, James, *The Holy Roman Empire*, MacMillan and Company, 1866. 212
[69]Wilson, Peter H. *Heart of Europe: A History of the Holy Roman Empire*. Harvard University Press, 2016. 144
[70]Painter, Sidney, *A History of the Middle Ages 284-1500*, The MacMillan Press LTD, 1973. 331

consistent economic policies. Occasionally, some cities benefited economically from this arrangement, but the lack of public law, courts of justice, and, most importantly, an emperor meant that the empire was headed toward a massive catastrophe.

These turbulent times also saw another "smaller" interregnum. The church was not immune to the constant feuds between the noblemen, and the conflicts transferred to the clergy. After Pope Clement IV's death, there were internal conflicts between the more notable cardinals and bishops. The temporary governance of the Catholic Church was collectively taken up by the College of Cardinals. This body was split equally between French and Italian representatives, leading to a deadlock between rival cardinals. There was no pope for almost three years, between 1268 and 1271. This was the longest *sede vacante* in history.[71] The extended duration of the conclave even resulted in the deaths of several cardinals. This further complicated the situation since the number of electors had decreased. In August 1271, the cardinals appointed a committee consisting of three representatives from each side to negotiate a settlement. However, the committee was unable to come to an agreement. As a result, one of the cardinals suggested looking outside their ranks for a solution. The elector-cardinals eventually agreed upon Teobaldo Visconti, Archdeacon of Liege, who had ties to France.

Although the decision was ratified by all the cardinals, it was more of a victory for the French faction. The church was experiencing a lot of disorder, and this encouraged Teobaldo, now known as Pope Gregory X, to act quickly to try to solve the problem. Although he himself could have benefited from the disorderly state the Holy Roman Empire was in, he found the disorganization generally unconstructive and realized the threat this chaos imposed. He instructed his subordinates and threatened the electoral princes to choose an emperor; otherwise, he would have to do it himself. Pope Gregory X also issued the papal decree *Ubi periculum* during the Second Council of Lyon in 1274, establishing regulations for the papal election, including measures to expedite the election process.[72]

---

[71] Latin for "with the chair [being] vacant," *sede vacante* is a term for the state without an acting pope upon his death or resignation.

[72] The title of the decree is taken from the opening words of the text, as is traditional for such documents. *Ubi periculum maius intenditur* can be translated to "where greater danger lies."

With the growing power of King Ottokar II of Bohemia and under the threat of Pope Gregory X, the electors realized that the chaotic state of affairs could not last much longer. King Ottokar II was a relative of Philip of Swabia and, therefore, posed a threat with his claim to the imperial throne through his Hohenstaufen roots. His intentions of expanding his jurisdiction into Babenberg lands (the eastern borders of the empire) alarmed the elector-princes. They swiftly went into action and appointed Rudolf, Count of Habsburg, as the new king of the Romans, ending the twenty-year-long period of unrest.

Rudolf's family gained prominence in the Alpine region, where he proved his military and diplomatic skills. His reputation contributed to his appeal as a candidate for the throne. The contested territories in Austria became a focal point of tension between Ottokar and Rudolf. The conflict culminated in the Battle of Marchfeld in 1278, where Ottokar suffered a decisive defeat, leading to his death.

Three men standing at the grave of an emperor; this depiction of the Interregnum can be found in Chronicon pontificum et imperatorum, written by Bishop Martin of Opava.

Rudolf didn't do much to improve the power of the German crown, although he successfully paved the way for a new great dynasty by marrying his son to the heir of Austria. He started his reign by reclaiming Hohenstaufen land that had been lost during the previous turbulent decades. During the course of his reign, he managed to recover the majority of the Hohenstaufen estates. His policy met some opposition in 1274 when a Diet in Nuremberg decreed Count Palatine of Rhine would be the judge in blood feud cases, diluting Rudolf's power in a way.

One of the main consequences of the crisis of the Great Interregnum was the official establishment of prince-electors as a legal entity that chose the next sovereign. The total number of cities grew tenfold, and they gained a certain degree of independence under the decisive interest of the local hegemon. Cities that managed to achieve more independence from the Holy Roman Empire emerged as new centers of economic power. Despite the political chaos, the increase of the empire's population was remarkable, as it almost doubled within a hundred years. Little did people know that the bubonic plague would soon wreak havoc across the whole of Europe.

Chapter 7: The Habsburgs Rise

The Habsburgs, a powerful German family, can trace their origins back to the 11th century. Their family name is derived from their ancestral seat at Habsburg Castle in Aargau (modern-day Switzerland). Initially holding minor titles, they gradually gained resources, and by the mid-13th century, they became serious contenders for the royal title. Through strategic marriages and alliances with other noble houses, such as the House of Luxembourg and the House of Burgundy, the Habsburgs expanded their influence and acquired vast territories across present-day France, Spain, the Netherlands, and the Holy Roman Empire.

Following the tumultuous and destructive events of the Great Interregnum (1254–1273), Pope Gregory X, who had recently been elected after a long period of instability in the church, urged the electors to choose a legitimate emperor to end the chaos in the empire.[73] Finally, after two decades of unrest, in 1273, it was agreed that Rudolf I, Count of Habsburg, would be elected as the king of the Germans. The second choice in the election was Ottokar II, King of Bohemia, but the electors preferred to choose a candidate who seemed to be a figure of mediocre power and influence in contrast to Ottokar II, who was fairly powerful and wealthy.

---

[73]There are some claims that the Great Interregnum started immediately after Emperor Frederick II's death in 1250, although it is generally described as following the death of his son Conrad IV in 1254.

During Frederick II's reign in the first half of the 13th century, the domestic power of the German king and the supremacy of the emperor suffered greatly.[74] During the turbulent times of the Great Interregnum, the German nobles seized power and prevented the restoration of the previous system of governance. The number of nobles who held almost complete control over their territories increased rapidly. Even a lord who held a small piece of land along the Rhine was often considered an independent prince.[75] Potential uprisings and unification among princes posed a great threat to the already reduced imperial authority.

Rudolf's election marked the beginning of a new era in European history. Known for his military expertise, Rudolf represented order and legitimacy in the empire, which helped calm tensions. His reign was, like Frederick II's, marked by issues and conflicts with the Papal States. Securing recognition from the pope was difficult due to the tarnished reputation of imperial rule in the preceding decades. Therefore, Rudolf's ability to exercise his imperial authority was somewhat affected.

Holy Roman Emperor Rudolf I as depicted in a 19th-century statue.
This file is licensed under the Creative Commons Attribution-Share Alike 3.0 Unported license.
This file is licensed under the Creative Commons Attribution-Share Alike 2.0 Germany license.
https://commons.wikimedia.org/wiki/File:Rudolf_Speyerer_Dom.JPG

[74]Painter, Sidney, *A History of the Middle Ages 284-1500*, The MacMillan Press LTD, 1973. 332-3
[75]Bryce, James, *The Holy Roman Empire*, MacMillan and Company, 1866. 229

The election of Rudolf as the king of Germany did not immediately lead to widespread uprisings, but it did have implications for the political landscape of the empire. Rudolf was able to consolidate Habsburg control in Austria by acquiring various lands and rights, which became the core of the Habsburg dynasty's power. However, he faced pressure from powerful nobles and bishops. During his time as ruler, he focused on taking advantage of his position to raise wealth by selling crown privileges for the benefit of his family. Despite this, the combined value of crown possessions increased thanks to the empire's successful economic development. Rudolf's success was fairly swift and surprising, indicating that the value of the positions of German king and Holy Roman emperor wasn't completely lost by the time Rudolf came to power.[76, 77]

The main changes during this period were the expansion of crown-owned lands and the response to the continuing emancipation of the ministeriales, who were granted full knight status and further immunities for royal monasteries.[78, 79] Monasteries were required to provide food and accommodation to royal representatives in the early 12th century, and this taxation was extended to royal towns as well. Rudolf developed on the structures initiated by Richard of Cornwall during the Great Interregnum and established bailiwicks to recover Austria, Carinthia, Styria, and Thuringia, which he claimed were vacant imperial fiefs.[80] The bailiffs relied on entrusting minor lords with the supervision of royal assets, shifting the basis of true imperial rule to rest on the king's direct possession of immediate fiefs as hereditary family lands.

Before his ascension to the throne, Rudolf's only rival was Ottokar II of Bohemia, who, despite losing the imperial election, still had claims to the Babenberg inheritance. Rudolf used his imperial powers to forcefully

---

[76] Bryce, James, *The Holy Roman Empire*, MacMillan and Company, 1866. 230

[77] It must be noted that Rudolf I was never crowned Holy Roman emperor, although he played a significant rule in reviving it.

[78] Ministeriales were unfree individuals who held military or administrative positions within the feudal system. They were not fully free knights and were bound to the service of a lord. Rudolf granted many of them the status of knights, allowing them to bear arms, thus expanding his influence over their positions.

[79] Wilson, Peter H. *Heart of Europe: A History of the Holy Roman Empire.* Harvard University Press, 2016. 555

[80] A bailiwick is usually the territory of a town or a monastery; it is under the jurisdiction of a bailiff, a legal officer responsible for overseeing the designated area.

resolve the issue in his favor in 1276, although Ottokar had certain princes backing him up and supporting his claim. Fortunately for the reigning emperor, Ottokar II died in the Battle of Marchfeld in 1278, and Rudolf continued to reign uncontested.[81]

Four years later, Rudolf assigned the Duchy of Austria to his sons at the Diet of Augsburg. The electors eventually agreed that Rudolf could employ his sons as dukes of Austria and Styria. There were still princes who supported Ottokar's family's claims and were wary of a king who was acquiring fiefs as personal property.

From that moment, the Habsburg dynasty was also known as the House of Austria. Nobles in other parts of the Holy Roman Empire still used lands that belonged to the emperor, but they also took advantage of their royal office to secure vacant fiefs for themselves.

After an eventful reign, Rudolf died of natural causes in 1291. Although he tried his best, he couldn't secure the succession to the German throne for his son Albert, largely due to the objections raised by Ottokar's son, King Wenceslaus II of Bohemia, as well as some other nobles.

Albert was known as Albert the One-Eyed, and there are various stories about how he lost his eye. One story claims he lost it in a battle, but some of his contemporaries believed that it could have been caused by an attempted poisoning, which he narrowly survived. Albert was not elected due to his poor attitude toward the electors and because of his "undignified looks." Despite this, Albert continued his father's efforts and tried to expand Habsburg influence and control in the Holy Roman Empire.

The prince-electors eventually chose Count Adolf of Nassau-Weilburg as the king of the Romans in 1292. Adolf's refusal to compromise with nobles over land disputes, which had reduced their support for him, led to a decline in his popularity. The electors did not plan to depose the king, but Adolf's policy toward Thuringia and his involvement in conflicts against nobles and electors made them join together to enforce their own interests. This occurrence was the first deposal of a sovereign by electors without papal involvement.[82]

---

[81]Wilson, Peter H. *Heart of Europe: A History of the Holy Roman Empire.* Harvard University Press, 2016. 557

[82]Wilson, Peter H. *Heart of Europe: A History of the Holy Roman Empire.* Harvard University

It is interesting to note that Adolf was not even excommunicated by the pope prior to being deposed. The reason behind this is that there was no convincing proof against Adolf since his election and coronation went uncontested. Despite this, the decision to let him remain in power remained highly controversial. Everything was eventually settled when Albert defeated Adolf in the Battle of Gollheim in 1298. By doing so, Albert regained the throne and immediately consolidated his possessions in Thuringia while also securing Bohemia, which had been left vacant after the death of Ottokar II.

Albert proved to be a competent ruler and gained more support from the imperial cities through effective economic measures. However, Albert was murdered by his own nephew, John, Duke of Swabia, in 1308. John was motivated by a desire for power and the inheritance of Albert's territories. After this event, John's name went down in history as John the Parricide. With the death of Albert, the House of Habsburg lost one of its most dynamic representatives, and his sudden death put an end to the efforts to keep the imperial crown in the family.

Albert's son, Frederick III of Austria, was supposed to succeed him, but the electors rejected the Habsburg heir. Also known as Frederick the Fair, he held the Austrian and Styrian duchies, but he couldn't manage to acquire the royal title.[83] Instead, Count Henry VII emerged as a better choice since he came from the affluent House of Luxembourg. Henry was voted by six of seven electors and was crowned by Pope Clement V in 1312. He unexpectedly died from malaria in 1313.

Henry's short reign and sudden death resulted in yet another tempestuous election. This was the first double election since the one that took place during the Great Interregnum. Henry's son, John of Bohemia, seemed too powerful for the electors, and the electors again neglected Frederick to become a candidate for the crown. The Habsburgs and Luxembourgs were evenly matched before the Habsburgs took the chance to proclaim Frederick the Fair as king in 1314 on the grounds that he was the legitimate heir. The very next day, the Luxembourgs elected their candidate as an anti-king, Louis IV of Bavaria, who was also supported by the powerful John of Bohemia. Frederick, however, still remained the first and right choice.

Press, 2016. 557
[83] This distinction helps differentiate him from Emperor Frederick III (1452–1493).

Louis was crowned at Aachen, while Frederick was forced to travel to Bonn for his coronation. Both tried to achieve the support of the imperial states, engaging in several years of bloody warfare for hegemony. Victory initially seemed to be within Frederick's grasp. The war for leadership ended in 1322 near the town of Mühldorf. Frederick was captured along with over one thousand nobles, but Louis didn't execute him.

In 1325, after a few years of imprisonment and due to the stubbornness of Frederick's brother, Leopold, Louis agreed to release Frederick under the Treaty of Rausnitz. With this act, Louis defused the unrest in the country caused by the war. He even recognized Frederick as a nominal co-king, while Frederick recognized him as a legitimate ruler. Strongly objected by the pope and prince-electors, Louis and Frederick ruled jointly.

With the Habsburgs' claim now weakened, a new rival emerged to counter Louis: Charles IV of Bohemia. Louis tried to acquire new territories, which inspired opposition from the Luxembourg elector, who foresaw Charles as the new king. Although the Habsburgs were displaced as kings by the Luxembourgs in 1308 and the Wittelsbachs of Bavaria in 1314, they were now in the front rank and were able to consolidate and expand their possessions in return for cooperating with the current monarch.[84]

Under the rule of the Wittelsbachs and Luxembourgs, the Habsburgs mostly ruled as dukes, primarily in Austria. The Habsburg dukes stayed loyal to Louis, while Pope Clement VI showed his support for Charles. Louis, in turn, remained politically powerful until his death in 1347. Louis's death occurred during a time of significant changes imposed by the devastating bubonic plague known as the Black Death. The death of an emperor coinciding with one of the deadliest pandemics in human history posed a great threat to the empire's stability.

Louis IV's sons supported Günther von Schwarzburg as a new rival king to Charles IV. Günther held the title briefly but faced difficulties in establishing widespread recognition. Just a few months after the election, Günther died, further complicating the political situation. Elector-princes eventually recognized Charles IV as the legitimate emperor.

[84]Wilson, Peter H. *Heart of Europe: A History of the Holy Roman Empire.* Harvard University Press, 2016. 610

Map depicting territories under different jurisdictions

- Land of the Luxembourgs
- Duchy of Austria under Habsburg rule
- Territory of Wittelsbach

The brothers of Frederick the Fair and their sons succeeded one another or ruled jointly throughout the next few decades. Rudolf I (not to be confused with Emperor Rudolf I) became the king of Bohemia but died at a relatively young age. Leopold I was, for a time, a co-ruler with his brother Frederick in the Duchy of Austria. Otto the Merry (sometimes referred to as Otto the Jolly), nicknamed like this in reference to the festive atmosphere of his court, took the title of duke of Austria. His focus shifted toward Bavaria after he married the daughter of Bavarian Duke Stephen. Albert II was a duke of Austria, Styria, and

Tirol at one point and was the closest to being crowned Holy Roman emperor. His sons, Albert III and Leopold II, ruled the Habsburg possessions together until 1379. Although always leaning toward it, none of the heirs to the Habsburg possessions reclaimed the imperial throne until the election of Frederick III in 1452.

Frederick was the son of Ernest, Duke of Austria. His father died in 1424, which made him the duke of Inner Austria. His uncle, Frederick IV, Duke of Tyrol, acted as regent since Frederick was only nine years old at the time of his father's passing. When Frederick was able to rule in his own stead, his younger brother, Albert, immediately asserted his rights as co-ruler, starting a long rivalry between the two. Frederick had to ward off the claims of his brother but eventually prevailed with the support of the Tirolean aristocracy.

Albert II (not Frederick's brother) became the Holy Roman emperor over a decade after marrying the duchess of Luxembourg, Elizabeth. She was the daughter of Holy Roman Emperor Sigismund, who died in 1437. Upon the death of Frederick IV, Frederick's uncle, in 1439, Frederick III became the regent for the duke's young heir, Sigismund.[85] In the same year, Albert II unexpectedly died of an illness, leaving Frederick to become the regent for his young heir, Ladislaus the Posthumous.

Ladislaus died at the age of seventeen in 1457, allowing Frederick to take over his inheritance. By this point, Frederick had already crowned himself king of the Romans, doing so in 1440. This coronation faced opposition from some electors who were dissatisfied with certain aspects of his rule. As a result, Frederick delayed his formal coronation and wasn't present at his own election in 1452. His regency in the lands under the jurisdiction of the Albertinian line was still viewed with suspicion.

Between the years 1444 and 1471, Frederick mostly stayed in his own lands, except in 1452 when he traveled to Rome to be crowned emperor. He would become the last Holy Roman emperor to be crowned in Rome.[86] Criticism arose after the emperor referred to himself

---

[85] He is known for becoming the king of Hungary at only three months old since he was born after his father Albert II's death, which granted him the nickname "Posthumous."

[86] His great-grandson Charles V was the last emperor to be crowned, although this was done in Bologna.

as Frederick III, the successor to Hohenstaufen rather than a successor to Frederick the Fair. In Vienna, during the year 1448, Frederick III signed an agreement recognizing Pope Nicholas V as the legitimate pope. In exchange, the pope restored the archbishop-electors of Trier and Mainz. The pope also confirmed the emperor's role in maintaining peace and order. The concordat was part of a broader effort by Frederick to stabilize the relationship between the Holy Roman Empire and the papacy. This concordat remained in force until 1806 and regulated the relationship between the Habsburgs and the Holy See.

Frederick also created an improved and centralized administrative institution known as the Imperial Chancery. This office was responsible for managing the Habsburg lands and records. The chancery played a central role in maintaining diplomatic relations with other European powers. It was responsible for treaties and agreements. This entity helped centralize power in the hands of the emperor and his advisors. Despite being known for his cautious and conservative approach to governance, Frederick did not actively pursue comprehensive reforms, instead focusing mainly on maintaining stability rather than implementing changes.

Tapestry depicting the coronation of Frederick III, wrongly attributing the pope in attendance as Pius II instead of Pope Nicholas V.

Frederick secured his own lands before turning his attention to the rest of the empire. However, he faced significant opposition from Austrian and Bohemian nobles. He abandoned his claims to disputed lands in 1458 but was soon embroiled in a dispute with his brother, Albert VI, over Austria between 1461 and 1463. In 1462, Albert raised an insurrection against Frederick in Vienna, and the emperor was besieged in his own residence. These conflicts forced him to move his court between various parts of the empire over the years. He lived in Graz, Linz, and Wiener Neustadt, where he is credited with the construction of a castle and a monastery.

Frederick opposed certain reforms proposed by Count Berthold of Henneberg, who emerged as a profound spokesman after becoming elector of Mainz in 1484. Henneberg wanted to exploit Frederick's desire to secure recognition of his son Maximilian as a successor. Frederick avoided direct conflict and held numerous discussions until electors accepted Maximilian I as king of the Romans in 1486. This was the first time in 110 years that a successor had been chosen during an emperor's lifetime. This was a positive sign that Henneberg and others genuinely wanted to work together with the Habsburgs after all.

Frederick retired to Linz in 1488 and left his son to manage the Holy Roman Empire. Since Maximilian could act as a mediator between princes and his father, the door to compromise was finally open. Maximilian continued this policy after Frederick's death in 1493.

The House of Habsburg was one of the most significant and longest-lasting royal families in European history. Over the course of centuries, they accomplished great feats and expanded their territories through strategic marriages and diplomatic prowess. For example, Maximilian I's union with Mary of Burgundy brought the Burgundian Netherlands under Habsburg control. The marriage of their son, Philip the Handsome, to Joanna of Castile further solidified Habsburg influence and united the Spanish and Burgundian territories.

Unfortunately, after Philip's death in 1506, Joanna began to suffer from mental health issues, earning her the nickname Joanna the Mad. Their son, Charles V, inherited all the lands from both sides of the family. From 1519 to 1556, during Charles's reign, the Habsburg Empire included the Holy Roman Empire, the Spanish Empire, the Austrian Empire, the Kingdom of Hungary, and many other territories. Charles V was fluent in Dutch, French, German, Italian, and Spanish, covering the most widespread languages of the empire. The Habsburg possessions were so vast that Charles had to appoint deputies and regents throughout his dominions.

In 1556, Charles shocked everyone when he decided to step down from his position as ruler and retire to the Monastery of Yuste in Spain. He divided his territory into two separate branches, each governed by representatives of the House of Habsburg. He officially abdicated the Holy Roman Empire and handed over the imperial scepter to his brother Ferdinand I, as appointed in the Diet of Worms back in 1521. During this period, Spain established a global empire through the colonization of the Americas. Charles V gave up the Spanish crown to his son, Philip II. The resources and wealth obtained from the Americas contributed to the rise of European global dominance and economic power.

The Habsburgs also played a significant role in the development of culture since they were major patrons of the arts. Vienna, as the capital of the Habsburg territories, became an important cultural center that attracted musicians, artists, and intellectuals. Notable figures, such as Wolfgang Amadeus Mozart, Ludwig van Beethoven, and Franz Schubert, found patronage and support from the royals. Charles V was known for his support of Titian, who painted several portraits of the emperor. The Habsburg Empire facilitated diverse cultural exchange, encompassing various ethnicities and cultures, which had a lasting influence on the regions involved.

The House of Habsburg's division was a momentous event in European history, leading to the formation of distinct branches that would shape the destinies of Spain and Austria in the forthcoming centuries.

Chapter 8: The Empire during the Reformation

Let's first focus a bit on the societal and cultural context in which the Reformation came about. During the late 15th and early 16th centuries, the Catholic Church experienced a significant increase in corruption. The church was characterized by moral decay, simony (the buying and selling of church offices), and the sale of indulgences (certificates that promised remission of sins).[87] Numerous clergymen were focused on wealth and political power. Rising interest in classical learning led scholars to explore ancient texts and the Bible in their original languages. The Renaissance resulted in questioning the official interpretation of the Bible. In addition, great discoveries, most notably the advancement of the printing press by German inventor Johannes Gutenberg in the mid-15th century, played a crucial role in the spread of new ideas.

Around 1500, the Holy Roman Empire underwent significant institutional changes known as "imperial reforms." However, these changes were not fully implemented, which led to a decline in both imperial and papal authority. These reforms also became closely intertwined with the problems within the church. As a result, the regulations were either rejected, accepted, or adapted by different national and local communities, which ultimately led to a reduction of

---

[87]Simonies were named after Simon Magnus, who is described in the Acts of the Apostles as having offered payment to two disciples of Jesus.

respect toward the emperor.

The political situation in Germany during this time foretold disaster. Unlike France or England, Germany was not a unified country but rather a collection of semi-independent states with similar dialects and cultural backgrounds, which all formed an empire, not a nation in the modern sense of the word. The emperor's influence was at an all-time low, which led to tensions and hostility toward the church, which was always allied with the Holy Roman Empire. As mentioned, the clergy managed to destroy its status and reputation via simony and the selling of indulgences. Despite some efforts made by Frederick III and his son Maximilian I, the situation remained unchanged throughout the first two decades of the 16th century.[88] Not only did the political arrangement look more anarchistic than monarchistic, but there was also chaos and disarray within societal norms and moral beliefs.

Maximilian I had an extremely strong character and was known for his bravery, strictness, and self-discipline. One of the last Holy Roman emperors to go by the example of his medieval predecessors, Maximilian I fought wars personally and even was deemed a bit reckless and over the top. On one occasion, he is said to have climbed to the top of the Cathedral of Ulm and walked to the very edge of the building, going around so that the frightened onlookers could see his reckless feat. Indeed, he is a personality worthy of a much more in-depth investigation that surpasses the narrow confines of this book.

Although Maximilian was a fairly fascinating character, he had his faults. He contributed to the accumulation of debt due to his unscrupulous, lavish, and irrational spending. His spending was so bad that the Italians referred to him as "Massimiliano di pochi denari" ("Broke Maximilian"). He was also unable to break the Venetian blockade and force his way to Rome, where he should have been crowned Holy Roman emperor. Although Pope Julius II granted Maximilian I the title of Elected Roman Emperor, Maximilian was the first Holy Roman emperor not to be crowned in Rome, which put an end to centuries of tradition.

In 1515, Pope Leo X was determined to complete the construction of the new St. Peter's Basilica in Rome. Indulgences were already a well-

---

[88]Maximilian had a plan to hold both the title of the pope and the Holy Roman emperor in 1511 but didn't succeed. This further emphasized the descending imperial and papal authority.

established method of funding, and he introduced new and more expensive ones in the papal bull issued the same year. According to the church's statement in the *Collectio de Judiciorum de Novis Erroribus*, published a few decades prior, "Every soul from Purgatory immediately goes to Heaven and is immediately released from any sin from the moment a believer puts six silver coins in the box to build the Church of St. Peter."[89]

Vatican obelisk and Saint Peter's Basilica in reconstruction, drawn shortly after 1523 by Marteen van Heemskerck.

https://commons.wikimedia.org/wiki/File:Maarten_van_Heemskerck_-_Santa_Maria_della_Febbre,_Vatican_Obelisk,_Saint_Peter%27s_Basilica_in_construction_(1.532).jpg

Although he was greatly opposed in Rome, Pope Leo X appointed Cardinal Albert of Brandenburg as the archbishop of Mainz, Magdeburg, and Halberstadt. Even though he was young and unqualified, Albert achieved supremacy over the three bishoprics with the help of a "self-willed agreement."[90] This act introduced the German public to the obvious abuse of positions achieved through simonies and

---

[89] *Collectio de Judiciorum de Novis Erroribus* is a collection of decisions of the Catholic Church over rising beliefs considered heretical; it was dismissed in Sorbonne as far as 1482 by an unnamed priest but continued to exist despite the censorship. Febvre, Lucien, *Martin Luther: A Destiny*, LDI, 1996. 75.

[90] Albert obliged himself to pay a fee in order to keep his claim to the bishoprics; he then borrowed the funds from a banker and paid off his title. Febvre, Lucien, *Martin Luther: A Destiny*, LDI, 1996. 72

indulgences. In the papal bull, Leo appointed Albert's bishoprics to give away half of their income for the construction of St. Peter's Basilica. The level of organization in this economic manipulation is nicely showcased in Pope Leo's alliance with Jakob Fugger, a successful banker who served as the pope's advisor. The pope recommended appointing Albert of Brandenburg to supervise the sale of indulgences in Germany. This campaign was led by Friar Johann Tetzel, who was notorious for his aggressive methods. Tetzel proposed a full remission of all sins to those who visited seven respected churches and paid a designated sum of silver after saying prayers. The abuse of position and the campaign in Germany shocked serious-minded believers, including Martin Luther, a theology professor at the University of Wittenberg in Saxony.

A few years prior, in 1510, Luther went on a pilgrimage to Rome. He walked for more than one thousand kilometers (seven hundred miles) over the snowy Alps, only to be dispirited by what he saw upon reaching his destination. This journey had a somewhat positive impact on Luther, allowing him to visit many holy sites and deepen his beliefs. However, the scenes he witnessed in Rome exposed the misuse of religious practices within the Catholic Church. In contrast to his native country, where the monks were known for their humility and modesty, he found wealthy priests indulging in drinking and gambling and engaging in relationships with women. These priests were found to be enriching themselves and living in luxury through the sale of indulgences.[91]

This had a profound effect on Luther. Upon his return to Wittenberg, he began sharing his thoughts with students during his lectures. He continued to preach to ordinary citizens, other theology professors, his superiors at the university, and even his foes. Gradually, he became a leader of a school of thought that challenged many of the Catholic Church's practices.

In response to the campaigns of Tetzel and Albert, a debate called *Disputatio contra scolasticam theologiam* was held under the auspices of Martin Luther. During the debate, Martin Luther presented ninety-seven theses, rejecting Scotistic doctrines, as well as Aristotelian metaphysics, logic, and ethics.[92, 93] Copies of the theses were sent to Luther's friends,

[91]Grand Larousse Encyclopedia, Vuk Karadzic, 1971-1973. 372
[92]Scotists were followers of Duns Scotus, a Scottish theology professor who tried to separate theology and philosophy in the 13th century.
[93]Febvre, Lucien, *Martin Luther: A Destiny*, LDI, 1996. 77

but he did not allow his students or other affiliates to print them for almost two years. In October 1517, Luther wrote better-structured theses and reduced the number to ninety-five. He attached the theses to a letter addressed directly to Archbishop Albert.

The calm and well-mannered tone of the letter and Luther's sincere intentions didn't mean this wasn't a bold move that could have bigger consequences. Luther's move became the first spark that started a fire that would soon take over Europe. The case was forwarded to the Roman Curia for judgment, although Pope Leo X remained uninterested in the matter at the time. On All Saints' Day, which falls on October 31st, many pilgrims came to Wittenberg to be granted forgiveness and to donate money to the church and crown. Luther saw this as a perfect opportunity to share his ideas. He posted his *Ninety-five Theses* on the gates of Wittenberg church.[94]

Wittenberg Castle Church as depicted in an illustration by Lucas Cranach the Elder in 1509.
https://commons.wikimedia.org/wiki/File:Schlosskirche_Wittenberg.jpg

---

[94]Luther titled the announcement *Disputatio pro declaratione virtutis indulgentiarum*—a disputation on the power and efficacy of indulgences.

The tensions between the pope and Luther rose as the papal nuncio (a diplomatic representative of the Holy See), Girolamo Aleandro, ordered the burning of Luther's books. In response, Luther, accompanied by his supporters, publicly burned the papal bull. The most significant challenge to imperial and Catholic goals came after the year 1517. The Reformation proved to be not only a religious movement but also a cause of political change. The uneven outcome of reformations and the already growing political and cultural differences led to the growth of more distinct national churches across Europe. This included the drift of some territories toward independence, such as Switzerland and the Netherlands.[95]

The decline in papal and imperial authority meant there was no single authority influential enough to judge Luther's beliefs. This resulted in acceptance, rejection, and adaptation of his beliefs by various local communities and clergies. It wasn't clear whether the emperor, princes, magistrates or the people should decide which version of Christianity was correct.

Luther's protest came at a very unpleasant moment for Maximilian I, who was in the middle of appointing his grandson, Charles V, as king of Spain and successor to the imperial throne. Charles won the election against the likes of King Francis I of France and King Henry VIII of England in 1519. Other circumstances ensured that Charles couldn't come to the Holy Roman Empire for two years after his coronation. Emperor Charles V was never a favorite among the Germans and was very attracted to the old faith. Two firm blocs began to form, and they were poised to start a bitter fight.

Luther wrote a grim letter to Pope Leo X in 1520 in which he expressed his anger and disappointment about what he had witnessed while in Rome. He showed sincere emotions, and he did not hesitate to tell his truth. "The Church of Rome, formerly the holiest of all Churches, has become the most lawless den of thieves, the most shameless of all brothels, the very Kingdom of sin, death, and hell; so that not even antichrist if he were to come, could devise any addition to its wickedness."[96]

---

[95]Wilson, Peter H. *Heart of Europe: A History of the Holy Roman Empire.* Harvard University Press, 2016. 200

[96]He wrote the letter in September 1520 as a response to Pope Leo's demand to renounce all of

Holy Roman Emperor Charles V's alliance with Pope Leo X was proven in the Diet of Worms in 1521.[97] Charles V called Luther and summoned him to the city of Worms, asking him to renounce his beliefs and accept the pope as a central figure within the church. Luther showed up and stubbornly disputed the old beliefs in front of the pope. As a result, he was proclaimed a heretic and excommunicated, along with everyone who supported him. Preaching these heretical beliefs was forbidden.

Luther survived only by the protection of Frederick the Wise, a Saxon prince who was hostile toward the church. Frederick escorted Luther to the security of Wartburg Castle in Eisenach, where Luther spent ten months translating the Bible into the German language. This work enabled a new perspective on the church to spread throughout Germany. Frederick had earlier forbidden the campaign of Friar Tetzel and Archbishop Albert in his territory. This was due to their role in lowering his revenues and depriving him of his income.

Luther's fallout resulted in the diversification of the initial movement in Germany. Soon, other reformers arose in other parts of Europe, most notably Ulrich Zwingli in Switzerland and John Calvin in France. The official excommunication of Martin Luther was published in January 1521 by Pope Leo X. Although the Reformation is usually considered to have started with the publication of the *Ninety-five Theses*, Luther's excommunication marked the definitive split between him and the church. Only a year after his expulsion, Luther returned to Wittenberg, where he asked Saxon elector-prince Frederick to title him as a servant of Christ and an Evangelist.

Contrary to Luther, who was surrounded by princes, noblemen, and scholars, some preachers found support among the poorer townspeople and peasants between 1521 and 1525. There were revolts by the peasantry in Franconia, Swabia, and Thuringia, known collectively as the German Peasants' War. These uprisings didn't receive approval from Luther, and many rebels laid down their weapons, feeling betrayed by him. Some preachers were executed at the Battle of Frankenhausen in 1525. This battle brought the revolution to a close, although radicalism continued to live on in the Anabaptist movement.

---

his writings.
[97]Wilson, Peter H. *Heart of Europe: A History of the Holy Roman Empire*. Harvard University Press, 2016, 202

Around 1526, a league of Protestant princes rose up against the Catholic Church. This league marked a period of tensions and conflicts with Charles V. The emperor had problems fighting with Francis I of France while also holding off the advance of Sultan Suleiman of the mighty Ottoman Empire.

This league was succeeded by the Schmalkaldic League, a league of Protestant princes focused on opposing the Holy Roman emperor. The league got its name from the town of Schmalkalden in Thuringia, where the Protestant princes met. Unlike previous formations, this league had a vastly better military to defend its interests. It was officially established by Philip I of Hesse in 1531. However, the Schmalkaldic League was weakened by internal divisions and scandals among its leadership.

The threats from outside of the empire, namely attacks by Sultan Suleiman and King Francis I of France, combined with the unification of his enemies inside the empire, forced Charles to conclude peace at Nuremberg in 1532. The Schmalkaldic League existed for fifteen years after that because Charles was too busy fighting wars with the French and the Ottomans. Inferior in military force and organization, the Protestant princes initially provided for their safety by forming leagues among themselves. Nevertheless, they began to look beyond their domain and found out that France was willing to join them in their fight against their common enemy, the Holy Roman emperor.[98] Francis I was a Catholic, and he even violently persecuted the Protestants at home, but he was smart enough to take advantage of the situation to further destabilize Charles's power and influence.

Charles was struggling, and he had to make peace with Francis, which was done with the Treaty of Crèpy in 1544. He also signed the Truce of Adrianople with Suleiman, allowing him to then focus on suppressing the Protestant resistance within the empire. Internal conflicts and scandals weakened the Protestants' position in Germany in the early 1540s. In 1542, Philip of Hessen and John Frederick I of Saxony invaded the Duchy of Brunswick, which earned them disapproval from the other princes. During this period of rising disagreements between the Protestants, sixty-two-year-old Martin Luther succumbed to illness and died in 1546.

---

[98]Bryce, James, *The Holy Roman Empire*, MacMillan and Company, 1866. 376

Charles built a coalition of princes against Philip of Hesse and John Frederick of Saxony, the most notable of whom was Prince Maurice of Saxony. Charles and his allies won a decisive victory in the Battle of Mühlberg in 1547. The triumphant emperor regulated religious issues with an imperial edict known as the Augsburg Interim in 1548. These regulations were only implemented in the southern German Protestant cities, proving that Protestantism was rooted deeper than Charles thought. It was agreed that if John Frederick surrendered, his life would be spared if he handed over his territory and electoral rights to Maurice. Charles didn't respect the agreement and imprisoned John Frederick and Philip of Hesse. This interim ended the Schmalkaldic War for a few years, but the Protestant princes, supported by Francis's successor, Henry II, were dissatisfied with the interim regulations. John Frederick was soon released from captivity, but Philip remained captive until 1552. The princes' main goal was to liberate him.

Since the league was dissolved and its leaders were captured, Charles rested and enjoyed his success. The North Germans, however, were still not giving up. They rose to arms and hurried through the Alps to surprise Charles and reach the imprisoned Philip.

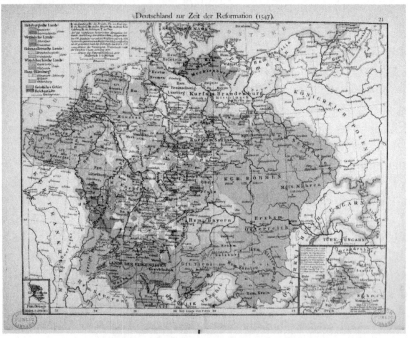

Map of the Holy Roman Empire in 1547 after the Augsburg Interim.
https://commons.wikimedia.org/wiki/File:Deutschland_im_XVI._Jahrhundert_(Putzger).jpg

The imprisonment of his father-in-law and the emperor's disregard of the Augsburg Interim estranged Maurice of Saxony from his imperial ally. As a result, Maurice went against the Augsburg Interim and landed on the side of the Protestants. In a momentary lapse of reason, Emperor Charles V sent Maurice to lead an army against Magdeburg, where Protestant princes were unifying. Maurice surprised the emperor when he switched sides to unite with the princes in the city. Their unified power was too great to defend against. The southern German cities that were still loyal to the emperor were quickly conquered in 1552. This victory forced Charles to flee to avoid capture. He appointed his brother, Ferdinand, King of the Romans, to sign a peace treaty and end the Second Schmalkaldic War. Because of Maurice's role in it, this war is also known as the Princes' Revolt.

In the city of Passau, King Ferdinand persuaded and coerced his opponents into agreeing with his proposals. The Peace of Passau in 1552 granted some freedoms to Protestants and ended Charles's hopes of religious unity. This treaty became the basis for the future Peace of Augsburg.

The Peace of Passau covered three main principles:

1. Ferdinand made an agreement on *cuius regio, eius religio.*[99] Though the phrase "he who rules decides the religion" was absent in the peace (it was coined by a professor in 1586), this was the basic underlying principle of both the Peace of Passau and the later Peace of Augsburg.[100] The principle provided for internal religious unity within the state. A prince's religion would become the religion of the state and its inhabitants, allowing other non-believers to leave freely.

2. The second principle covered the status of ecclesiastical states. If a prince-bishop changed his religion, he would have to relinquish his rule, allowing the state to, for example, elect a Catholic successor.

3. The third principle is known as Ferdinand's Declaration, and it exempted princes and some cities from the requirement of

[99] *Cuius regio, eius religio* is Latin for "whose realm, their religion."
[100] Wilson, Peter H. *Heart of Europe: A History of the Holy Roman Empire.* Harvard University Press, 2016, 212

religious uniformity.[101] This was a concession aimed at a few imperial cities where Lutherans and Catholics coexisted.

The Peace of Passau led to the religious division of Germany between Catholic and Protestant princes. Since Charles's interim solution didn't satisfy anyone, he ordered a general diet in Augsburg in 1555, at which various states would meet to discuss religious problems.

Since the last effort to produce religious uniformity by violence had failed, an armistice was agreed upon in 1555 in Augsburg. It lasted for more than sixty years, but there was still mutual fear and suspicion. This agreement entered history as the Peace of Augsburg.

Representatives of the German estates negotiating the religious peace at the Augsburg conference.
https://commons.wikimedia.org/wiki/File:Peace-of-augsburg_1555.jpg

Between 1554 and 1556, Charles gradually divided the Habsburg Empire and the House of Habsburg between a senior Spanish line and a German-Austrian line. He gave more sovereignty in Spain and the Indies to his only surviving son, Philip II, as well as Flanders and Naples. Charles completed his abdication in 1556 and passed the imperial scepter in favor of his brother Ferdinand. The succession was recognized in 1558 by the electors and by the pope in 1559.

---

[101]Ferdinand implemented it at the last minute; Emperor Charles didn't order it.

Ferdinand ruled the Holy Roman Empire capably and managed to leave things as he found them. His son, Maximilian II, who was personally inclined toward Protestantism, was unable to quench the flame of political and religious hatred still present within the empire and the church. Germany remained divided into two factions and was further away than ever from unification. There was no recognized center of authority.

Although a period of coexistence and peace was achieved, the slow but gradual expansion of Protestantism beyond the boundaries of Lutheran and Catholic cities destabilized the settlement. The Peace of Augsburg, in a way, presented opportunities for those who sought to weaken central authority that had already been weakened. The peace was far from perfect and only attempted to address the immediate consequence of the rift between Protestants and Catholics. In the end, the religious conflicts of the 16th century contributed to the devastating Thirty Years' War, which saw further religious and territorial divisions within the Holy Roman Empire. During the fifty years of forced respect between factions, the underlying unrest expanded to a war of grand proportions. This war became one of Europe's deadliest conflicts.

Chapter 9: The Thirty Years' War and the Peace of Westphalia

The Thirty Years' War was a major European war, its consequences projecting far into the future and even influencing our modern lives. In a way, the Thirty Years' War was a war of religion, one of many that happened in Europe around that time, but it was also fought because of economic, political, and ethnic reasons.[102] However, the religious nature of the war was certainly prevalent. As we've seen, early on in the Holy Roman Empire, there was a sort of oscillation between the church as the holder of the empire and the church being the enemy of the empire. For hundreds of years, popes and emperors were able to find solutions to the never-ending struggle between the spiritual and worldly realms.

However, once the authority of the Catholic Church came into question via the Protestant Reformation, even more serious problems started to emerge. The authority of the Habsburgs, who were allied with the Catholic Church, was also undermined.

It all started in Bohemia, where Protestantism had already set foot. In 1618, open conflicts between Bohemian Protestants and the Catholic Habsburg monarchy started. But there is a whole historical introduction to the war in Bohemia. Around 1606, in Donauwörth (in Bavaria,

---

[102]Wilson PH. The Causes of the Thirty Years' War 1618–48. The English Historical Review. 2008 Jun 1;123(502):554-86.

though at the time Donauwörth was a free imperial city),[103] a city populated by mostly Protestants, the city council refused to allow Catholic processions in the city.[104] Minor scuffles broke out, and each time, the Catholics were refused access to the city. Finally, Emperor Rudolf II ordered an armed takeover of Donauwörth, which was carried out by the head of Bavaria, Maximilian. Donauwörth lost its status as a free imperial city and was gradually integrated into the Bavarian administration. Protestants were refused the right to worship.

This event alarmed normal citizens and the Protestant aristocrats, who faced the prospect of losing some territories that had recently been taken away from the Catholic Church and given to them. The heads of Palatinate, Brandenburg, Kulmbach, Baden-Durlach, Hessen-Kassel, Württemberg, and Ansbach were all Protestant and decided to form a sort of union to counter the atrocities against the Protestants in the Holy Roman Empire. Soon enough, the Catholics formed their own league, vowing to defend the interests of their religion.

The next important precipitator of the Thirty Years' War happened when the head of the Jülich-Cleves-Berg region died without an apparent heir. The two main claimants were both Protestants and had temporarily entered into a sort of alliance because the emperor wanted to give the region to another contender due to political reasons. The two Protestant claimants started rallying their forces to repel the forceful retake of what both of them perceived to be their own territory. The emperor, in turn, sent his cousin, Leopold, to take over the region and bring it under direct imperial control. However, Leopold's forces were too few, and his progress into the region was blocked. The two Protestant contenders were soon supported by some very powerful people, such as King Henry IV of France. Leopold, on the other hand, expected support from the Spanish Crown. A hereditary conflict threatened to turn into a real all-out European war.

Tensions were building between Protestants and Catholics. In 1610, King Henry IV of France was killed by an assassin. This event quelled the tension around the hereditary question of Jülich-Cleves-Berg, as the Protestant side saw its support dwindle. However, the animosities

---

[103]Free imperial cities were directly responsible to the court; they weren't governed by regional authorities.

[104]Mortimer G. The Origins of the Thirty Years' War and the Revolt in Bohemia, 1618. Springer; 2015 Aug 11.

between Protestants and Catholics were such that they were bound to spring up elsewhere.

In Bohemia, the Catholics started suppressing the rights of Protestants, pressuring them to convert to Catholicism. Distinguished Protestants lost their positions in the administration in spite of assurances made by the Habsburgs. In 1618, the most notable Protestants of Bohemia were scheduled to meet with the imperial delegation and discuss their precarious position. The meeting between Protestants and imperial envoys was strained and tense at best. Not happy with the answers, one of the Protestants drew out his pistol and fired in the air. Two of the four imperial envoys were particularly despised by the Bohemian Protestants, William Slavata and Jaroslav Martinic. The other two were expelled from the negotiation room, and the Protestants were alone with what they perceived to be their arch-enemies.

The Protestants recounted all the misdeeds committed by Slavata and Martinic against the Protestants. The crowd became angrier and angrier, and people soon started shouting and calling for punishment. The two, as well as a secretary, were thrown out of the window. In spite of falling down around fifteen meters, they survived. Martinic and the secretary suffered minor injuries, and Slavata earned himself an injured head. All three managed to escape the assailants.

Defenestration of Prague by Johann Philipp Abelinus.
https://commons.wikimedia.org/w/index.php?curid=1431443

Martinic returned to Germany, where he told everyone about the violence he and his colleagues had been subjected to. Back in Bohemia, people were arming themselves against the imperial army, quickly amassing around four thousand men.[105] Now the tables had turned, and the Protestants started pressuring the Catholics in Bohemia.

The Habsburg government wasn't exactly in the position to quickly suffocate this rebellion. The government was almost always in heavy debt, and its forces were guarding the borders of the vast empire. The Bohemian rebels had some time to establish their rule. In 1618, Frederick of Palatine, a German Calvinist, accepted the Bohemian crown, becoming the most hated person among German Catholics. In 1619, the leader of the revolt, Thurn, ordered the Bohemian forces to enter Moravia, a Czech region that vacillated between the imperialists and the Protestants. Thurn then turned toward Vienna, besieging it in 1619. However, the Spanish reinforcements aiding the Holy Roman Empire stopped this siege. Another army friendly to the Bohemian Protestants, Mansfield's mercenary army, was defeated by the imperialists, which prompted Thurn to retreat to Bohemia. The Bohemians once again besieged Vienna in 1620 but to no avail. The military actions, coupled with the approaching winter and general neglect of the army, exhausted the Bohemian soldiers, who had been decimated by illnesses, the cold, and a lack of basic necessities.

This set the stage for the ultimate and decisive breakdown of the rebellion in Bohemia. In 1620, the imperialists finally crushed the revolt, though seeds of dissent were already sown across Europe. It wouldn't take too long before conflicts sprang up elsewhere.

Thirty Years' War: The Belligerents

It has to be emphasized right from the start that the Thirty Years' War was neither a purely religious nor purely political war. On the one hand, we had France, the Netherlands, Scandinavian kingdoms, Bohemia, Swiss cantons, German Protestant princes, Venice, and Hungary. This was a very diverse bunch. France, for instance, was, strictly speaking, a Catholic country, and Venice was as well, at least to a certain extent, but they chose to side with the Protestants due to their animosities with the Catholic Habsburgs of Germany and Spain.

---

[105]Mortimer G. The Origins of the Thirty Years War and the Revolt in Bohemia, 1618. Springer; 2015 Aug 11.

On the other hand, we had the Catholic Holy Roman Empire, Spain, the Italian states, and Poland.[106] The Thirty Years' War also had economic and constitutional roots. The modern age had begun, and feudalism was on its deathbed. However, Europe didn't simply go from the medieval age to modernism in a fortnight. This was a gradual process unevenly spread throughout Europe. There were centers of all kinds of reforms, and there were centers of conservatism. Generally speaking, in the Thirty Years' War, one side (Bohemia, the Netherlands, Scandinavia, etc.) sought more political, religious, and economic changes, while the other side (the Holy Roman Empire, Spain, Poland, etc.) sought to minimize these changes and go back to the feudal system as much as possible. In a way, religion was in the midst of this whole process. Protestantism was the religion of wealthy, educated middle-class citizens, who incidentally were the most likely to seek profound changes to the nations they lived in.

However, things weren't so simple. France, a Catholic kingdom with a significant Protestant minority, sided with the Protestants due to its animosities toward Spain and Germany. The Italian states, arguably among the most developed in Europe at the time, sided with Spain and Germany, helping them to maintain a political system far from that which was enjoyed by the many semi-independent Italian states. Venice is a good example. It was on very bad terms with Spain and the Holy Roman Empire during the Thirty Years' War despite sharing the same Catholic faith.

The Thirty Years' War: Delving Deep into the Chaos

After the defeat of Bohemia, the Catholics in Germany were emboldened and threatened to repress the liberties enjoyed by Protestants in regions like Saxony and Brandenburg. Denmark's king, Christian IV, had interests in these regions since he was closely tied with the aristocrats who were holding these areas. Even though Christian IV was a Protestant, he wasn't really interested in joining the conflict until he realized his lands in Saxony and Brandenburg were in danger because the Catholic League wanted to get a hold of them.[107]

---

[106]POLIŠENSKÝ, Josef V. The Thirty Years' War. Past & Present, 1954, 6: 31-43.
[107]Lockhart, Paul Douglas. Political Language and Wartime Propaganda in Denmark, 1625–1629. European History Quarterly, 2001, 31.1: 5-42.

The Danes attempted to take control of what they perceived to be their land in Germany in 1625. However, they were soon overpowered by the imperial army and were forced to retreat. Danish pride was salvaged thanks to the fierce resistance of their troops, but Christian IV never managed to salvage his own reputation despite signing a fairly favorable peace with the Holy Roman Empire in 1629.

Sweden's intervention in Germany was much more successful than the Danish intervention. This addition to the Thirty Years' War came about thanks to the diligent diplomatic work of the French. Heralded by the devious and covetous Cardinal Richelieu, the French were able to quell the animosities between Poland and Sweden and then convince Sweden to join the war against the Holy Roman Empire. In a little bit, we'll deal with the French side and the incredibly interesting Cardinal Richelieu.

The Swedes were pushed to act due to their expansionist territorial interests. They were also sincerely worried about their religious freedoms if the Holy Roman Empire succeeded in completely suppressing the Protestants. The Swedes were frightened seeing the Danes almost completely crushed by the Germans.[108]

With the entrance of Sweden, the conflict that started in Bohemia and moved toward the northern part of Germany, close to the Baltic Sea and Denmark, was becoming more and more international. The war was drawing France further into conflict with both Spain and the Holy Roman Empire. Sweden managed to sway the city of Magdeburg to join its cause in 1631 and took important positions in Pomerania.

The siege of Magdeburg was an important event in the Thirty Years' War. The Swedes were en route to Magdeburg, where a friendly politician was installed. However, the Swedish forces weren't quick enough to capture Magdeburg, and the city fell to the imperial forces on May 20th, 1631. The imperialists proceeded to sack the town, which only furthered the Swedish cause within the Holy Roman Empire. Numerous princes were persuaded to join the Swedish side.

The head of the region of Saxony, John George, immediately allied with King Gustavus Adolphus of Sweden. The two men combined their armies to form a formidable force that was able to face imperial might.

---

[108]Davis TM. The Swedish Intervention: How the Thirty Years' War Became International. The Alexandrian. 2017;6(1).

The combined armies of Saxony and Sweden faced the imperialists near the village of Breitenfeld. Interestingly, the Swedes were able to defeat the imperialists despite the Saxons fleeing the battlefield shortly after the battle began. This win drew even more support for the Swedish cause within the Holy Roman Empire. In 1632, the Swedish forces were able to take vast areas in the north of Germany largely unopposed.

Gustavus Adolphus by Johann Jakob Walter.
https://commons.wikimedia.org/w/index.php?curid=21330817

The Battle of Lützen shows just how fierce the battles during the Thirty Years' War were. The Swedes narrowly won, but their king, Gustavus Adolphus, was killed in the battle. A mass grave from this battle has been recently found, and it was filled with skeletons of those who were presumably killed during the battle. It provided a good opportunity to learn about the type of people who participated in the battle, such as how old they were.[109] It was found that the youngest victim in this pit was around fifteen years old, while the oldest was around fifty. Most had died due to trauma inflicted by projectile-based weapons (artillery or guns), but there were some signs of injuries inflicted by blades, which were still widely used in the 17th century. The Swedish Army was somewhat more numerous than the Germans, though only slightly.

---

[109] Nicklisch N, Ramsthaler F, Meller H, Friederich S, Alt KW. The face of war: Trauma analysis of a mass grave from the Battle of Lützen (1632). PLoS One. 2017 May 22;12(5):e0178252.

Prior to the fighting, the forces of Gustavus Adolphus, aided by the Saxons, faced the German forces led by Albrecht von Wallenstein on a foggy evening, which made navigation almost impossible and forced the two armies to wait a bit before attacking each other. Around noon, German reinforcements arrived in the form of cavalry units, which managed to push the Swedes back and inflict heavy damage. From then on, the battle degraded into a sort of free-for-all. Visibility was once again impaired due to the heavy smoke caused by gunfire, making any attempt to gain control over the armies futile. We can only imagine how hard it was to establish control over different units of a large army in the 17th century, let alone doing so with low visibility.

Gustavus Adolphus virtually lost his way on the battlefield and ran into enemy cavalry. He was promptly killed. Curiously, the death of Gustavus Adolphus didn't completely destroy morale among the Swedish troops, and the Germans didn't even believe that the Swedish king had been killed. The German reinforcements were also late to the battlefield, arriving late at night and only having the option of covering the retreat of their comrades, who were going back to Leipzig. The Swedes remained on the battlefield and were able to recover the body of their king.

The losses were heavy on both sides, with both armies losing around five thousand or six thousand troops. The Swedes, however, took the moral victory, proving to the whole of Europe that the Holy Roman Empire and the Catholic Church were far from invincible.

This precipitated the final entrance of France onto the scene of the Thirty Years' War. Seeing the fruits of its previous endeavors, France, led by Cardinal Richelieu, entered the war in 1635. Let's focus for a while on this great personality since he was so important for the developments of the Thirty Years' War and long ago entered European popular culture through works such as *The Three Musketeers*.

Richelieu's beginnings were fairly modest. Although a minor noble by birth, Armand Jean du Plessis (later 1st Duke of Richelieu) saw many hardships in his early life in the French region of Poitou. The region and indeed a majority of France at the time of his birth (1585) had been ravaged by years of conflict between Protestant Huguenots and French Catholics.[110]

---

[110]Rehman I. Raison d'Etat: Richelieu's Grand Strategy during the Thirty Years' War (May 2019).

Violence wasn't only around Richelieu; it was also deep within his family. Richelieu's father, François, had been drawn into a blood feud when he was only seventeen years old. Following an age-old feud between Richelieu's family (du Plessis) and their neighbors, the Maussons, over who was going to control their local church, François's uncle was murdered. François then carefully prepared a vendetta on the head of the Mausson family, murdering him in an ambush. François made his way up the French royal hierarchy thanks to his ruthlessness and discipline, becoming an important commander and executioner to French Kings Henry III and Henry IV.

Cardinal Richelieu by Philippe de Champaigne.
https://commons.wikimedia.org/w/index.php?curid=93172350

However, François died when Richelieu was only five years old, leaving his wife to attend to the family in exceedingly bitter times. Richelieu vacillated between a military or ecclesiastical career before finally settling on a career in the church when he gained control over the Bishopric of Luçon. Richelieu's older brother became a monk within the Order of Carthusians, giving up the ecclesiastical position in Luçon, which the family originally designated for him.

Thanks to Richelieu's cunning, self-discipline, and superior intellect, he slowly rose through the ranks. Inspired more by the strategy of Machiavelli than classical works (Richelieu was proficient in Greek and Latin), he knew who to side with. For instance, he made his way in the entourage of Concino Concini (the king's minister), who was much admired by the queen-mother, Marie de' Medici. Concino promoted Richelieu to the position of secretary of state in 1616, but he wasn't able to do much else for Richelieu as he was assassinated the year after. Assassination was a very frequently utilized instrument at the time. In the decades leading to Richelieu's ascension, four French kings were assassinated, which greatly contributed to the general chaos in the state, something that plagued Richelieu's conscience and pride as a Frenchman.[111]

France's chaos and perception of overall decline, especially in comparison to the Habsburgs, who managed to almost completely surround France, precipitated Richelieu's rise and his use of devious tactics. Unlike what's been painted in the works of popular culture, Richelieu wasn't necessarily or exclusively a power-hungry man who would do anything to increase his influence and dominance. Richelieu was, first and foremost, a nationalist. He wanted to bring France back to its glory. This desire to reinvigorate the already-hurt French national pride nicely explains Richelieu's "the ends justify the means" tactics. Richelieu, for instance, knew that France was too weak to directly confront either Spain or the Holy Roman Empire at the time of his ascension to the post of chief minister (the king's closest advisor and second-in-command). So, he labored against the Habsburgs by inciting other kingdoms to fight them and succeeded by drawing Sweden into the conflict. This not only gave France more time to recover from decades of calamity and internal strife, but it also weakened France's main adversary.

While Sweden was battling Germany, France was busy building a powerful navy that could pose a significant threat to the Spanish. Richelieu also built a powerful diplomatic force. Numerous French emissaries crossed Europe, seeking to draw new players into the conflict against the Habsburgs and plant seeds of disunion within Spain and Germany. Secessionist movements within Catalonia and Portugal received significant backing from France, as did rebellious German

[111]Ibid.

princes.

In France, Richelieu managed to suppress the Huguenots, a large Calvinist-Protestant group in France, with a combination of reason and ruthlessness. Initially moderate toward Huguenots and supporting their conversion to Catholicism via rational persuasion, as the years went on, Richelieu became a supporter of more direct military confrontation with the Huguenots, which resulted in the final victory of French Catholics in 1627 when the Huguenot-held city of La Rochelle was taken over. Richelieu was also a far-sighted policy-maker. In 1626, the destruction of most French fortresses (other than those situated on the frontiers) was ordered in an attempt to unify the French nobility by discouraging internal strife. Counts, princes, and dukes were less likely to fight one another if they didn't have a safe place to withdraw to. Also, in 1627, Richelieu ordered a ban on duels, which decimated the elite and complicated the question of succession and inheritance.

The cardinal constantly persuaded people within France that a war against Spain, implicit or explicit, was more favorable to France than an alliance. Those who wanted to side with France and put an end to its alliance with Protestant nations were swayed by a powerful propaganda machine. Numerous writers cried out against Spain's inhumane treatment of indigenous populations. Richelieu himself was a proponent of the more humane and enlightened approach to assimilating indigenous peoples to the French way of life in the French colonies. The Spaniards' Catholicism, one of the few ties between Spain and France, was thus undermined. Anyone who favored an alliance with Spain on the pretext of Catholicism received this strong counterargument.

Finally, Richelieu opened Académie Française and Imprimerie Royale, two institutions that were under the careful control of the royal court.

These and other sophisticated methods covered the period of France's involvement in the Thirty Years' War known as the *guerre couverte* ("covert war"). In 1635, Sweden had significantly weakened the Holy Roman Empire. Richelieu recognized it was high time to turn the *guerre couverte* into *guerre ouverte* ("open war").[112] The Swedes couldn't face the Habsburgs on their own. In spite of fighting valiantly, they suffered several defeats. Now, the Swedes and the Dutch were pushing

---

[112]Ibid.

France to come out of the shadows and face the Spaniards and Germans out in the open. By this time, France had amassed up to 200,000 men, a formidable army in comparison to what the French had been able to put out just a few decades prior.

However, the *guerre ouverte* wasn't simply a war of arms. It was also a war of propaganda. Just prior to the breakout of hostilities, Richelieu sent numerous envoys across Europe, hoping to shape the narrative about the impending conflict. France, of course, was displayed as a protector of the most noble virtues. Spain was an evil colonialist kingdom that was only superficially Christian. In 1625, the "barbaric" Spanish troops attacked the French town of Trier, slaughtering anyone who was found within. The Spaniards were painted as a people who constantly vied for supremacy in Europe, threatening the basic liberties of European populations.

In 1635, France was somewhat successful, defeating the Spaniards at Les Avins. A year later, the Holy Roman Empire was drawn into the conflict, and France faced a war on two fronts. This proved to be disastrous for France, as its enemies managed to penetrate deep into its territory, coming to around sixty kilometers of Paris. This was probably the lowest point in Richelieu's career. He plunged into a deep depression. He seemed to give up and even attempted to resign. However, this wasn't allowed, and Richelieu was quite literally forced to move on and get back to work. General mobilization was ordered in France, led by the fiery and warlike King Louis XIII. Luckily for the French, the invading forces in the north of France were dangerously overextended, and pushing the forces back to Germany wasn't as hard as it might have initially seemed.

A protracted war favored the French, who had more people than Spain or the Holy Roman Empire. The French managed to gradually push the Spaniards and Germans back and even crossed into their territories. However, the unseasoned French troops weren't used to fighting in foreign territory. Richelieu solved this problem by hiring mercenaries to fight abroad and keeping the bulk of domestic forces in France.

We chose to focus on France's role in the Thirty Years' War because it decidedly shifted the balance of power away from the Habsburgs and toward the French-Protestant bloc. Although the Germans finally managed to bring religious peace to their empire in 1635 via the Peace of Prague, they weren't able to provide significant backup to their Spanish allies and mostly dealt with constant Swedish incursions into northern Germany. France kept the Spaniards busy and also caused some problems for the imperial army. The French provided enough space for the Dutch to harness a powerful fleet and constantly harass the Spaniards, whether in Europe or in faraway colonies. The Dutch were able to slow down Spanish naval actions in the colonies, constantly breaking their supply chain.

Although the power of the Swedes was very much weakened by 1634, prompting France to enter the war, in a few years' time, the Swedes managed to recover and got back on the road to victory. In 1639, the Swedes were once again in Germany, penetrating deep into enemy territory from their Baltic Sea bases in northern Germany. After reaching Saxony, their advance was halted near Chemnitz by Saxon forces led by Rodolfo von Marzin. The Swedes inflicted a crushing defeat on the Saxons in 1639, opening the way to Bohemia.

The Dutch naval victory at Downs (the English Channel) over the Spanish navy in 1639 and another victory close to the Brazilian coast of Pernambuco in 1640 contributed to the breakdown of Spanish naval dominance and marked a symbolic breakdown of Spanish power. These losses heralded Spanish problems back home; Portugal and Catalonia both started to revolt over harsh living conditions and heavy taxation.

For several years, there was heavy fighting, and the German and Spanish forces were slowly ground down. Swedish intervention was once again crucial. Lennart Torstensson led the Swedish Army to multiple victories in 1642, most importantly in the Second Battle of Breitenfeld, where around ten thousand imperial soldiers perished. Leipzig soon fell under Swedish pressure.

By now, it had become clear that the Habsburgs, for all intents and purposes, had lost the war. The only question was how much territory they would lose. Not even the war between Sweden and its neighbors, Norway and Denmark, could seriously slow down the Habsburgs' breakdown. In 1646, the French and Swedes were able to further grind down the imperialists, with Saxony deciding to exit the war.

The end of the war didn't come without some surprises. Richelieu's successor, Cardinal Mazarin, sought to strike a secret agreement with Spain in which Spain would completely withdraw its claims to Catalonia, now occupied by the French. In return, the French would give up the

Netherlands to Spain. This secret offer went public, angering the French and prompting the Dutch to seek a separate peace with the Spaniards in 1647.

In 1648, understanding that the end of the war was near, the Swedes tried to take over Prague, hoping for bountiful loot and an even more favorable position for the peace talks that were going on at the time. They were unable to capture the whole of Prague, but they did raid numerous castles, monasteries, and buildings, taking historical documents and works of art.

The peace talks that were going on during the siege of Prague in 1648 are now known as the Peace of Westphalia. The war that started in 1618 in Prague ended with the siege of Prague in 1648. The Dutch negotiated a peace separately with Spain in what is today known as the Treaty of Münster; the peace between France and the Holy Roman Empire was also achieved in Münster. The Swedes settled matters with the Holy Roman Empire in the Treaty of Osnabrück.

The most important consequences of the Peace of Westphalia are the following:

1. The Netherlands gained de facto independence, though some areas, such as Antwerp, would still remain under Spanish command.

2. The Holy Roman Empire vowed to grant religious freedom to its subjects; more specifically, Lutherans gained virtually the same rights as Catholics. Calvinism was officially recognized as a legal religion.

3. The *cuius regio, eius religio* of the Passau and Augsburg talks from one hundred years before was reaffirmed with an important addition: subjects didn't have to follow their leaders' religious denominations.

4. The defining date for the division of ecclesiastical property was January 1ˢᵗ, 1624. All changes that had been made after this date had to be reverted.

5. France received territories around Toul, Verdun, and Metz, as well as Pignerol in Italy and Decapole in Alsace.

6. Sweden received Western Pomerania, a region in northern Germany.

7.   The Swiss received formal independence.[113]

The Peace of Westphalia marked the final end of the Holy Roman Empire. The German states became heavily fragmented, just as they had been during the end of the Roman Empire. The Habsburgs still enjoyed power in Spain and Austria. They managed to cross into the modern age, although the same cannot be said for the Holy Roman Empire.

It cannot be emphasized enough that the Holy Roman Empire never managed to get out of the medieval age. It was a medieval state *par excellence.* Because the leaders were unwilling or unable to transform the Holy Roman Empire into a modern empire, it failed under the burden of religious, political, and economic conflicts brought about by the modern age. The Germans, divided across a multitude of smaller or bigger states led by quasi-feudal lords and divided by religion, with varying dialects and different traditions, had to wait a bit longer to be unified under the banner of one nation, one language, and one culture.

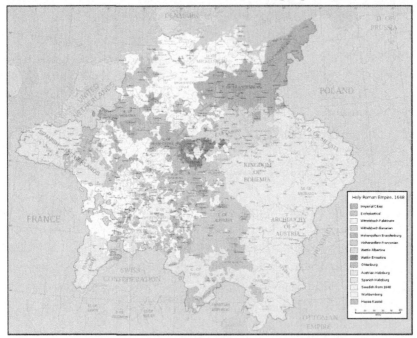

The Holy Roman Empire after the Peace of Westphalia.
Astrokey44, CC BY-SA 3.0 <http://creativecommons.org/licenses/by-sa/3.0/>, via Wikimedia Commons https://commons.wikimedia.org/w/index.php?curid=1612601

[113] GROSS, Leo. The Peace of Westphalia, 1648–1948. *American Journal of International Law,* 1948, 42.1: 20-41.

Conclusion

After the Peace of Westphalia, the Holy Roman Empire slowly but surely sank to the bottom. With France gaining the upper hand, heralded by King Louis XIV and his incredibly long reign, and the Habsburgs slowly building a stronghold in Austria that would eventually become their next empire, the remnants of the Holy Roman Empire were left to continue to deteriorate. In the 150 years that followed the Peace of Westphalia, the Holy Roman Empire formally and symbolically had an emperor who could only dream of power and influence enjoyed by the likes of Barbarossa or the early Habsburgs.

But like all great empires, the Holy Roman Empire met its end. It was destroyed by the short-lived French Empire and the brilliant Napoleon Bonaparte. Holy Roman Emperor Francis II had the incredibly challenging task of keeping the empire afloat while facing French revolutionary zeal channeled by Napoleon's strategic genius.[114] Unable to counter Napoleon on the battlefield, Francis II attempted a symbolic counterattack. In 1804, he proclaimed the formation of the Austrian Empire.

It's hardly a coincidence that earlier in 1804, Napoleon proclaimed himself the first French emperor. It became clear to Francis II that the days of the Holy Roman Empire were numbered after seeing Napoleon's initial successes. By forming the Austrian Empire, where the

---

[114] EVANS, Robert; WILSON, Peter (ed.). The Holy Roman Empire, 1495-1806: A European Perspective. Brill, 2012.

Habsburg dynasty would have the strongest foothold, Francis II ensured that his family would continue enjoying imperial might even after the dissolution of the Holy Roman Empire. Moreover, the Austrian Empire, in a way, inherited the allure and pride of the Holy Roman Empire, becoming the most powerful German state in the 19th century, at least before the formation of the German Empire in the late 19th century.

In the aftermath of the Battle of Austerlitz in 1806, Francis II formally dissolved the Holy Roman Empire. It's likely that Francis II was afraid that Napoleon would crown himself the Holy Roman emperor and take this opportunity away from him. The Confederation of the Rhine (West Germany, roughly speaking) was established by Napoleon, who was the confederation's protector.

The Holy Roman Empire, always oscillating between fragmentation and unity, finally ceased to exist. However, the German people's desire to unite under a single banner would live on. The breakdown of the French Empire would leave enough space for the Germans to regroup and regain their strength, culminating in the proclamation of the German Empire in 1871.

It is hard to describe the importance of the Holy Roman Empire in history. With the decline of the Byzantine Empire in the late medieval age, the Holy Roman Empire took the banner and led Europe, allowing for the slow but progressive rise of Western Christianity and cultures. The Holy Roman emperors acted as protectors of the church, without which there wouldn't have been such things as the Renaissance or the modern age. It may sound a bit surprising that we're establishing a sort of continuity between the modern period and the Holy Roman Empire by pointing out the empire's role in protecting the church. After all, the church did many bad things during the medieval age. However, the church also allowed for cultural endeavors and ensured at least some kind of education.

The Roman Church provided much-needed structure in a world riddled by war, disease, and famine. It also provided a structure against which to rebel. New kinds of people emerged from deep within the Holy Roman Empire, people willing to criticize the church and make the world a better place. Without the Holy Roman Empire, we likely wouldn't have had the Reformation, and without the Reformation, Europe and the world would be totally different. The Protestant ethic, according to German sociologist Max Weber, resulted in a special kind of economic system that we refer to today as capitalism.

The Holy Roman Empire was also, in a way, a reflection of the German people's desire to unite under a single state. However, the very idea of the Holy Roman Empire was supra-ethnic and supra-national; it's much older than the idea of nations, which is the basis of the modern world order. The Holy Roman Empire was, strictly speaking, a medieval empire based on much older Roman ideals, and for that reason, it was deemed to fail as Europe reached modernity. This meant that other nations that were quicker to grasp the power behind nation-states and adopt republican constitutions, such as France and the United Kingdom, took primacy in Europe and the whole world in the 19th century.

When the Germans finally awoke from their sleep and unified in 1871, they realized they had to fight with an increasingly powerful France and the UK. What the Germans perceived as a lack of balance within Europe ultimately led to World War I in 1914. Although some believe this war was caused by the assassination of Archduke Franz Ferdinand in Sarajevo, it was, in fact, an extremely long process that started with the dissolution of the Holy Roman Empire.

The Holy Roman Empire, therefore, is instrumental in understanding some of the events that happened relatively recently, such as the Great War. It's also well known that Hitler referred to his state as the Third Reich, a successor of the Holy Roman Empire (the First Reich) and the short-lived German Empire (the Second Reich). Hitler's obsession with German history and the events of the 19th and early 20th centuries that saw German influence in Europe dwindle prompted him to promote a radical ideology meant to bring Germany back into the spotlight of history. It's not a coincidence that one of the greatest military offensives in history was called Operation Barbarossa.

Fortunately, the German nation outlived Hitler's perverted vision of the Third Reich, and it continues to exist today, leading Europe into a new age.

If you enjoyed this book, a review on Amazon would be greatly appreciated because it would mean a lot to hear from you.

To leave a review:

1. Open your camera app.
2. Point your mobile device at the QR code.
3. The review page will appear in your web browser.

Thanks for your support!

Here's another book by Enthralling History that you might like

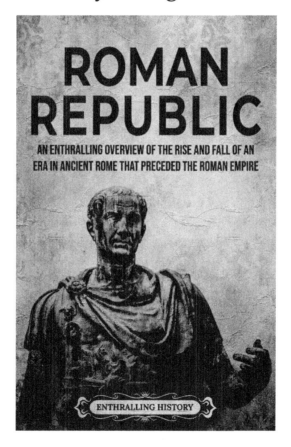

Free limited time bonus

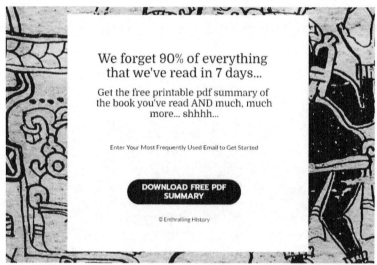

Stop for a moment. We have a free bonus set up for you. The problem is this: we forget 90% of everything that we read after 7 days. Crazy fact, right? Here's the solution: we've created a printable, 1-page pdf summary for this book that you're reading now. All you have to do to get your free pdf summary is to go to the following website: **https://livetolearn.lpages.co/enthrallinghistory/**

Or, Scan the QR code!

Once you do, it will be intuitive. Enjoy, and thank you!

Bibliography

Heather, Peter. Empires and barbarians: The fall of Rome and the birth of Europe. Oxford University Press, 2010.

Contreni, John J. "Introduction:" The Merovingian Kingdoms", 450-751." French Historical Studies 19, no. 3 (1996): 755.

Barbero, Alessandro. Charlemagne: Father of a continent. University of California Press, 2018.

Joranson, Einar. "The Dissolution of the Carolingian Fisc in the Ninth Century." (1936): 545-547.

Merlo, Brian. "Pope John X and the End of the Formosan Dispute in Rome." PhD diss., Saint Louis University, 2018.

Ganshof, François Louis. Feudalism. Vol. 34. University of Toronto Press, 1996.

MacLean, Simon. "History and politics in late Carolingian and Ottonian Europe: the Chronicle of Regino of Prüm and Adalbert of Magdeburg." In History and politics in late Carolingian and Ottonian Europe. Manchester University Press, 2013.

HAUFF, Andrea. The Kingdom of Upper Burgundy and the East Frankish Kingdom at the beginning of the 10th century. *History Compass*, 2017, 15.8: e12396.

BACHRACH, David Stewart. Milites and Warfare in Pre-Crusade Germany. *War in History*, 2015, 22.3: 298-343.

BACHRACH, David. Exercise of royal power in early medieval Europe: the case of Otto the Great 936–73. *Early Medieval Europe*, 2009, 17.4: 389-419.

BACHRACH, David S. Early Ottonian Warfare: The Perspective from Corvey. *Journal of Military History*, 2011, 75.2.

WILSON, Joseph. Holy Anointment and Realpolitik in the Age of Otto I. 2015.

Robbie, Steven. "Can silence speak volumes? Widukind's Res Gestae Saxonicae and the coronation of Otto I reconsidered." Early Medieval Europe 20, no. 3 (2012): 333-362.

Poole, Reginald L. "The names and numbers of medieval popes." The English Historical Review 32, no. 128 (1917): 465-478.

Grabowski, Antoni. "Liudprand of Cremona's papa monstrum: The Image of Pope John XII in the Historia Ottonis." Early Medieval Europe 23, no. 1 (2015): 67-92.

Brook, Lindsay. "Popes and Pornocrats: Rome in the early middle ages." Foundations 1, no. 1 (2003): 5-21.

Roach, Levi. "The Ottonians and Italy." German History 36, no. 3 (2018): 349-364.

Osborne, John. "The dower charter of Otto II and Theophanu, and the Roman scriptorium at Santi Apostoli." Papers of the British School at Rome 89 (2021): 137-157.

Welton, Megan, and Sarah Greer. "Establishing Just Rule: The Diplomatic Negotiations of the Dominae Imperiales in the Ottonian Succession Crisis of 983-985." Frühmittelalterliche Studien 55, no. 1 (2021): 315-342.

Zeller, Jules. L'empire germanique et l'Eglise au Moyen-Age: les Henri. Vol. 3. Didier, 1876.

Morrison, Karl F. "Canossa: A Revision." Traditio 18 (1962): 121-148.

De Mesquita, Bruce Bueno. "Popes, Kings, and endogenous institutions: The Concordat of Worms and the origins of sovereignty." International Studies Review 2, no. 2 (2000): 93-118.

Roche, Jason T. "King Conrad III in the Byzantine Empire: a foil for native imperial virtue." (2015).

Weiler, B. (2009). The King as judge: Henry II and Frederick Barbarossa as seen by their contemporaries. In Challenging the boundaries of medieval history: the legacy of Timothy Reuter (pp. 115-140).

Velov, Ivana. Literary and Historical Interpretation of Frederick Barbarossa's Conquest of the Italian Communes: Analysis of the Events and Personalities Described in the Novel "Baudolino" by Umberto Eco. ДИПЛОМАТИЈА И БЕЗБЕДНОСТ, 249.

FRANKE, Daniel. From Defeat to Victory in Northern Italy: Comparing Staufen Strategy and Operations at Legnano and Cortenuova, 1176-1237. Nuova Antologia Militare, 2021, 2.5: 27.

Friederich A. Warlord or Financial Strategist: Frederick Barbarossa. Johns Hopkins University. 2022 Nov 10;3(1).

Frederick I. The crusade of Frederick Barbarossa: The history of the expedition of the Emperor Frederick and related texts. Ashgate Publishing, Ltd.; 2010.

Bryce, James, *The Holy Roman Empire*, MacMillan and Company, 1866. 232

Painter, Sidney, *A History of the Middle Ages 284-1500*, The MacMillan press LTD, 1973. 326

Holmes, George, *The Oxford History of Medieval Europe*, Oxford University press, 1988. 225

Wilson, Peter H. *Heart of Europe: A History of the Holy Roman Empire.* Harvard University Press, 2016, 557

Grand Larousse encyclopedia, Vuk Karadzic, 1971-1973. 372

Febvre, Lucien, *Martin Luther: A Destiny*, LDI, 1996. 77

Wilson PH. The Causes of the Thirty Years War 1618-48. The English Historical Review. 2008 Jun 1;123(502):554-86.

Mortimer G. The Origins of the Thirty Years War and the Revolt in Bohemia, 1618. Springer; 2015 Aug 11.

POLIŠENSKÝ, Josef V. The Thirty Years' War. Past & Present, 1954, 6: 31-43.

LOCKHART, Paul Douglas. Political Language and Wartime Propaganda in Denmark, 1625–1629. European History Quarterly, 2001, 31.1: 5-42.

Davis TM. The Swedish Intervention: How the Thirty Years War Became International. The Alexandrian. 2017;6(1).

Nicklisch N, Ramsthaler F, Meller H, Friederich S, Alt KW. The face of war: Trauma analysis of a mass grave from the Battle of Lützen (1632). PLoS One. 2017 May 22;12(5):e0178252.

Rehman I. Raison d'Etat: Richelieu's Grand Strategy During the Thirty Years' War (May 2019). Texas National Security Review. 2019.

GROSS, Leo. The peace of Westphalia, 1648–1948. *American Journal of International Law*, 1948, 42.1: 20-41.

EVANS, Robert; WILSON, Peter (ed.). The Holy Roman Empire, 1495-1806: A European Perspective. Brill, 2012.

Printed in Great Britain
by Amazon

56000080R00076